D1083172

DU BOIS'S TELEGRAM

Du Bois's Telegram

Literary Resistance and State Containment

JULIANA SPAHR

Harvard University Press

Cambridge, Massachusetts
London, England
2018

First printing

Library of Congress Cataloging-in-Publication Data

Names: Spahr, Juliana, author.
Title: Du Bois's telegram : literary resistance and state containment / Juliana Spahr.
Description: Cambridge, Massachusetts : Harvard University Press, 2018. |
Includes bibliographical references and index.
Identifiers: LCCN 2018012877 | ISBN 9780674986961 (alk. paper)
Subjects: LCSH: American literature—Political aspects. | Politics and literature—
United States. | Nationalism and literature—United States.
Classification: LCC PS65.P6 S63 2018 | DDC 810.9/358739—dc23
LC record available at https://lccn.loc.gov/2018012877

CONTENTS

DU BOIS'S TELEGRAM

Introduction

IN 1956, W. E. B. Du Bois was invited to attend the Congress of Black Writers and Artists, a conference organized mainly by Alioune Diop (editor of the journal *Présence Africaine*) to support and strengthen the production of literature by black writers. The conference promised to be significant, with many luminaries in attendance. Léopold Senghor, Aimé Césaire, Jacques Rabemananjara, and Richard Wright were all on the planning committee. And, as Diop would note in his eventual "Opening Address," the congress was designed to be a second Bandung (the Bandung Conference, a large gathering of representatives from recently independent or soon to be independent African and Asian nations to discuss political self-determination and establish nonaggression and noninterference understandings, had been held the year before in Indonesia): "To-day will be marked with a white stone. If to the non-European mind the Bandoeng meeting has been the most important event since the end of the

War, I venture to assert that this first World Congress of Negro Men of Culture will be regarded by our peoples as the second event of the decade."[1]

Du Bois had been among those invited to attend the congress, but he was unable to do so because the U.S. government had revoked his passport the previous year.[2] So instead of attending, Du Bois sent a telegram to be read at the conference: "Any Negro-American who travels abroad today must either not discuss race conditions in the United States or say the sort of thing which our state Department wishes the world to believe. The government especially objects to me because I am a socialist and because I belief in peace with Communist states like the Soviet Union and their right to exist in security."[3]

Du Bois's concerns were not far-fetched. Nor were they paranoid. While there is nothing to indicate that Du Bois knew this at the time, the Americans who were invited to attend as presenters—included were Horace Mann Bond, Mercer Cook, John Davis, James Ivy, William Fontaine, and Wright—were funded by the American Committee on Race and Class (sometimes called the Council of Race and Caste in World Affairs), a CIA front group.[4] In addition, all had agreed to file reports to the Congress for Cultural Freedom, another CIA front group created to covertly launder funds from the CIA into various cultural diplomacy projects, when they returned.[5] Cook, a professor at Howard University, would eventually become the director of African programming for the Congress for Cultural Freedom in the 1960s.[6] It was Wright though, not Cook, who had a large influence on the composition of the American delegates. Wright was on the team that assisted Diop with the organization of the Congress of Black Writers and Artists. He had missed the first few meetings because he was out of town and when he finally attended he realized that there was talk of Du Bois being invited. Hazel Rowley, Wright's biographer, quotes a dispatch that the American embassy in Paris sent to the State Department that mentioned that Wright had "on his own initiative" contacted the embassy because he was worried that "the Communists might exploit the Congress to their own ends."[7] He requested assistance from the embassy in suggesting "possible American negro delegates who are relatively well known for their cultural achievements and who could combat the leftist tendencies of the Congress."[8] Wright "returned to the Embassy on several occasions to discuss ways in which they could 'offset Communist influence.'"[9] This was not Wright's first experience as an informant. In 1954 he named Communist names at the American consul in France.[10] And it would not be his only attempt to block Du Bois. Du Bois's name, with Paul Robeson's, was put forward as a desired member of the executive council when Diop was assembling his Société Africaine de Culture the following year. Wright worked with John Davis to pressure Diop by threatening to abandon plans for a Society for African Culture in the United States if the national chapters were not allowed to nominate the members of the Société.[11] When Diop succumbed, the U.S. chapter nominated Duke Ellington and Thurgood Marshall.

It is impossible to know what Du Bois would have said if he had attended the congress (or if he would have attended if he could have). But we do know that the U.S. delegates who attended spent much of their time arguing about anticolonialism with many of the fellow attendees. John Davis, for instance, complained about the negativity of Aimé Césaire's talk and argued with his claims that American blacks, because of racism, occupy an "artificial position" that "can only be understood within the context of a colonialism."[12] According to Davis, American Negros do not "look forward to any self-determination."[13] Wright gave a talk at the second *Présence Africaine* Congress of Black Writers and Artists in support of colonialism as a form of modernization, one that claimed that the "Western world helped, unconsciously and unintentionally, to smash the irrational ties of religion and custom and tradition in Asia and Africa! THIS IS MY OPINION, IS THE CENTRAL HISTORICAL FACT!" and also one that argued that "Nehru, Nkrumah, Nasser, Sukarno, and the Western educated chiefs of these newly created national states must be given *carte blanche* right to modernize their lands without overlordship of the West and we must understand the methods they will feel compelled to use. . . . Yes, Sukarno, Nehru, Nasser and others will use dictatorial methods to hasten the process of social evolution and to establish order in their lands."[14] James Baldwin in "Princes and Powers," his report on the congress, mentioned that Du Bois's telegram and Wright's talk (which he called "strange") "increased and seemed to justify the distrust with which all Americans are regarded abroad, and it made yet deeper, for the five American Negroes present, that gulf which yawns between the American Negro and all other men of color."[15]

In this book I attempt to take Du Bois's telegram seriously, to think about the ramifications of what was obvious to him in 1956—that the government's interest in literature should not be taken lightly—and trace the impact of this interference into the turn of the twenty-first century. Or another way to put this, I began this book with an old question about how to understand the vexed and uneven relationship between literature and politics. This relationship has been much debated, much declaimed, much mocked and denied too. No one is more convinced than writers of literature that literature has a role to play in the political sphere, that it can provoke and resist. They assert it all the time.

While often theoretically sophisticated, much of this assertion is fairly ahistorically optimistic. Also, much of it lacks analysis of the structural issues: literature's stubborn relationship to and reliance on the state, the impact of private foundations, of higher education, of a highly centralized multinational publishing industry and a localized, decentralized small press culture. All these forces skew and manipulate literature's political valences in especially intense and unique ways in the post-1945 United States. At the same time, those who tear down this optimism (and many a writer denies the relationship between literature and politics) often do so not by pointing to these structural conditions of literary production, but by arguing that politics makes for bad literature, makes propaganda, all the while ignoring the constant use of "apolitical" literature as propaganda through U.S. cultural diplomacy. Scholars echo their versions of similar arguments. On the one hand, an Adorno-esque sense that "now is not the time for political works of art; rather, politics has migrated into the autonomous work of art, and it has presented itself most deeply into works that present themselves as politically dead, as in Kafka's parable about the children's guns, where the idea of nonviolence is fused with the dawning awareness of an emerging political analysis."[16] On the other, Lorde-esque optimistic narratives about the resistance of literature, about its ability to decolonize, about its revolutionary potential. My conviction is that in order to understand the relationship between literature and politics, one has to attend to specific examples and the nuances of history that shape these specific examples.

I chose as my specific example the literature of the turn of the twenty-first century (from the 1990s to the contemporary). I chose this example mainly for personal reasons: I am a writer of literature in addition to a writer about literature and this literature of the turn of the century was the literature that had led me to writing. I have been moved by various works of literature that were published in the 1990s. Moved not just in my heart but also moved into writing and out into the streets at the same time. It was through the socialities that surrounded this sort of poetry that I began attending street protests. And it was through poetry's socialities again that I attended various prosovereignty protests when I moved to Hawai'i in the mid-1990s. And it was a pattern that continues to define my life today. I showed up at Occupy Oakland with a bunch of poets whose sociality overlapped with the socialities of ultraleft anarchist and communist scenes. This literature has, in short, a special place in my heart. So I began with a scholarly desire to notice what was unique about this moment and a desire to defend this literature as aesthetically beautiful, as meaningful.

But it was not just my heart and feet that led me to take turn of the century literature as my example. I had also spent many years discussing the politics of this literature before I began this book. The question of what literature might do politically defined the graduate seminars that I took when I was at the State University of New York at Buffalo in the early 1990s. Much time was spent in those graduate seminars arguing the line by W. H. Auden that "poetry makes nothing happen."[17] Our discussion in these seminars was notably ahistorical and very much indebted to the thinking that was the anthology *The Politics of Poetic Forms* (Charles Bernstein, the editor of that anthology, taught many of these seminars). By which I mean we were literally thinking hard about how avant garde literary strategies, such as the use of fragmented language, might be a political strategy, might be resistant. Was it true, as Bruce Andrews claimed, that there is "a social, political dimension in writing," one that might embrace "concern for a public, for community goods, for overall comprehension & transformation"?[18] Is there really, as he stated, "in recent years with this work, a conception of writing as politics, not writing about politics"?[19] Is that conception at all meaningful or recognizable? Is Bernstein's equation in *Contents Dream* that "Language control = thought control = reality control" true? And if so, can language actually be "decentred, community controlled, taken out of the service of the capitalist project"?[20] When Erica Hunt, again in *The Politics of Poetic Form,* writes first of how "writing itself cannot enlarge the body of opposition to the New Wars" and yet then continues on, almost in direct contradiction, with the optimism that "it only enhances our capacity to strategically read our condition more critically and creatively in order to interrupt and to join," we debated if this was at all possible.[21]

The belief that language writing might provide some meaningful answers to these questions was probably unique to SUNY Buffalo. And it would have had a lot to do with who was teaching there in the 1990s: not just Bernstein, but also Susan Howe, Robert Creeley, and Joan Retallack (who was a visiting professor for a year). Otherwise, language writing was an odd place to put so much pressure on this old question of the relation between literature and resistance. In *The Matter of Capital,* Chris Nealon notes how much of the scholarly attention to this work, he references in particular work by Charles Altieri and Marjorie Perloff, presented a "powerfully depoliticizing language for poetry in the 1980s and 1990s."[22] And of all the poetries that make political claims at the last half of the twentieth century, language writing had fairly weak ties to street politics, was in no way connected to the various antistate (often cultural nationalist) uprisings that were happening in the late 1960s and into the 1970s, and was often even openly hostile to them. Barrett Watten, for instance, in his discussion of the Free Speech Movement at Berkeley, calls the Black Panther Party "at best symbolic (taking guns into the California state capital) and at worst contradictory (the invocation to armed insurrection; the demand for a school breakfast program)."[23] Ron Silliman in "Poetry and the Politics of the Subject," dismisses writing by "women, people of color, sexual minorities, the entire spectrum of the 'marginal'" as "conventional."[24] Perloff, whose scholarly work has long argued for the importance of language writing, frequently in her work sets language writing in opposition to more racially concerned writing. Dorothy Wang's *Thinking Its Presence* begins with a detailed exploration and critique of this opposition and as she does this she notes that often "Perloff explicitly frames the choice as one between 'passionate' and 'literary' writing by famous named authors, all white, and an undifferentiated mass of unliterary writing by nameless minority authors."[25] And within the field of the seminars we took—which because it was Buffalo and because it was the "Poetics Program" were all in contemporary U.S. poetry in the modernist tradition— we never turned to Native American poets such as Simon Ortiz or Hawaiian poets such as Haunani-Kay Trask for support. Even as Trask has throughout her career been attentive to culture as a part of the Hawaiian sovereignty movement, calling her own writing "in the Hawaiian grain and, therefore, against the American grain . . . exposé and celebration at one and the same time," and "a furious, but nurturing aloha for Hawai'i."[26] Many of us acted as if the modernist tradition excluded writing that had direct connections to thriving culturalist and anticolonial movements of the time (meaning, to list just one obvious example, we basically did not read the literature written in French in Africa in the 1950s and 1960s). And even as many of us read some of the poets associated with Umbra—Lorenzo Thomas read at Buffalo several times and I would include him among the atypical and very small canon of writers that defined the program during those years—I never heard anyone mention how, as James Edward Smethurst puts it in *The Black Arts Movement,* "Marxism, nationalism, or some combination of the two, was central to the lives of many of the members," how Umbra was something that splintered from the black nationalist group On Guard for Freedom, or how those associated with Umbra went together to the 1963 March on Washington and Art Bergers's claims that they showed up armed.[27]

It would be easy to attribute this to bad thinking, to notice that I would not have turned to either anticolonialism or cultural nationalists for support in these debates about the Auden line because I was generally not involved in anticolonial movements at the time and did not see my writing as having to take a stand on the continuing legacies of colonization that are imperial globalization. I (wrongly) did not see myself as part of that legacy of colonialism that is imperial globalization. While I respected the concerns of anticolonial struggles, the form that my respect took was almost comic. It was basically a refusal to belittle their goals with a claim of alliance on my part. I knew I wrote from a different sort of First World privilege, even as I tried to write against this, both as a scholar and as a poet. But I could not figure out how as a writer of empire to not only be against empire in my writing and / or to consider my writing influenced by the writing of anticolonial struggles. There was some (white) ally talk at the time but the role of allies was mainly limited to how they might avoid appropriation. Rather than figuring out how to become an accomplice, I became avoidant.

This was obviously naïve. No writing escapes being a part of anything. And the Mohawk Nation, the very same one where

James Thomas Stevens (a poet who was often around Buffalo at the time and whose work I discuss in this book) grew up, was right down the road. When I left Buffalo and moved to Hawai'i in 1995, it was again poetry's socialities and prosovereignty literatures that pointed out the naïvete of this to me. But at the same time it is also naïve to see my avoidance as innocent. I was thinking in the way that the State Department and the liberal foundations that worked with the State Department wanted me to think. But at the time I did not have that thought. This book is in part an autobiography about how I came to have that thought, how I came to realize that if I wanted to understand the peculiar challenges that face writers who want to write against the empire in which they find themselves I could not understand this without also understanding that poetry is "stubbornly national" as T. S. Eliot calls it in "The Social Function of Poetry."[28]

So first a formal observation: from the late 1980s to the turn of the twenty-first century something interesting happened. Some of the more provocative literatures written in English began to include languages in addition to English; actually not just some, but an unusual amount. Some of these writers included, through appropriation and quotation, languages that were unrelated to them in terms of heritage or location, or perhaps even fluency. M. NourbeSe Philip, for instance, used Portuguese, Spanish, Dutch, French, German, and English—the languages of nineteenth-century European colonialism—in her work. Other writers included heritage languages that could easily be presumed to be a constitutive part of their subjectivity. But even as they did this, most of these writers at the turn of the century, instead of saying, as Gloria Anzaldúa did in her 1987 *Borderlands/La Frontera: The New Mestiza,* "I am my language," said something more complicated about this relationship between identity and language,

something about how they were not their language.[29] For instance, Myung Mi Kim, when writing of the disquieting disorientation brought on not just by immigration but also by globalization
in her book *Commons,* wrote a series of questions that well reflects the concerns of these works as something other than constitutive of her personal subjectivity: "What is English now, in
the face of mass global migrations, ecological degradations, shifts
and upheavals in identifications of gender and labor?"; "What are
the implications of writing at this moment, in precisely this
'America'?"[30] These questions about what it means to write in
English—not only the questions that Kim asks but also questions that she almost asks, questions about what it means to
write in the expansionist language of empire—haunt and define some of the most interesting literature written at the turn
of the century.

In order to understand this cluster of works that include languages other than English, I turned to Benedict Anderson and
Pascale Casanova. In *Imagined Communities,* Anderson writes of
language, "What the eye is to the lover—that particular, ordinary
eye he or she is born with—language—whatever language history
has made his or her mother-tongue—is to the patriot. Through
that language, encountered at mother's knee and parted with only
at the grave, pasts are restored, fellowships are imagined, and
futures dreamed."[31] Anderson's argument is that there are three
obvious ways that print-language produces the imagined community that is nationalism: it creates unified fields of exchange (so
people realize through the development of print-capitalism that
they are part of a linguistic community); it fixes language (so
readers in the twenty-first century can read writing from the seventeenth century); and it differentiates them and thus makes
some languages more powerful than others. Literature, as it is

written in languages, creates, Anderson notes, a "special kind of contemporaneous community" through poetry and songs.[32] Literature, in short, is not only one of the places where nationalism manifests itself, but it carries a relation to nationalism in the very materials of its composition.

Casanova adds to Anderson's observations when she tells a long history of the use of linguistic variance in literature in *The World Republic of Letters*. She reads this variance as a way that writers refuse to imagine the national community, refuse to restore the past, imagine easy national fellowships, or dream of futures. In her telling, "language is not purely a literary tool, but an inescapably political instrument as well, it is through language that the literary world remains subject to political power."[33] The world republic of letters that Casanova describes is one where there is a nationalist literary tradition, one where "national writers turn their back on the wider world and devote themselves to literary conservatism."[34] It is a literature that is written in the language of the state, the standard language. And then there is at the same time, and in opposition, a literature written in resistance to this national tradition. This literature deliberately avoids the standardized language of the state. Dante is a classic example here. While in exile, he turns from Latin to write in "Italian." And Casanova's study is full of additional examples including the English romantics and many of the modernists. She does not mention language poetry, but she could have.

So if nationalism is, as Anderson argues, dependent on print cultures (even if literature is just one of the print cultures that he locates as crucial to feelings of national belonging) and if some literature, as Casanova adds, attempts to contest the feelings of national belonging through atypical language practices, then this literature in English that includes other languages is provocative, engaged. After Anderson, after Casanova, after Kim, I pursue a related series of questions. If standard-language literature has played a special role in establishing the imaginary communities of nationalism, then might nonstandard-language literature be understood as proposing other sorts of imagined communities? Are these communities meaningful? Is it possible in the contemporary moment for literature to be meaningfully antinational or even just other than national? I more or less answer yes to the first question; more or less no to the second and third.

As I previously stated, much of this discussion about literature's ties to resistance movements, whether by poets in blog posts or by scholars in theory speak, tends to see resistance in literature as static. Little attention is given to how literature might be a part of these moments at one moment and then not at another. There are, for instance, many excellent scholarly studies on how various literatures develop their aesthetic concerns in dialogue with resistance movements. Alfred Arteaga noted in *Chicano Poetics:* "After the historical-political and historical-racial facts, the border and Indianness figure into the matter of Chicano subjectivity, into chicanismo, as sites and occasions of cultural interaction."[35] Smethurst, in *The Black Arts Movement,* charts the "complicated and often contradictory network of cultural activists and institutions" that "incubated African American cultural nationalism, revolutionary nationalism, and the multicultural movement."[36] Urayoán Noel, in *In Visible Movement,* notices how "poetry, and performed poetry in particular, was central to the Puerto Rican Movement of the 1960s and 1970s, from the Young Lords to the Nuyorican Poets Café and beyond."[37] Robin D. G. Kelley's *Freedom Dreams,* with its focus on freedom and love as revolutionary, is an unusually inclusive (and beautifully optimistic) study of these movements: "In the poetics of struggle and lived experience, in the utterances of ordinary folk, in the cultural products of social movements, in the reflections of activists, we discover the many different cognitive maps of the future, of the world not yet born."[38] Dale Smith, in *Poets beyond the Barricade,* notices how "from the Vietnam War to the occupation of Iraq, a rhetorical poetics that is motivated by social and political issues of local and global significance shapes how we understand civic protest, public formation, ideological narratives, and cultural history, asking us to look more closely at specific public environments and social relations."[39] But most of the studies that celebrate this relationship as revolutionary barely address why these ties so often fail to be revolutionary for long, fail to grow, or merely maintain solidarity. This book attempts to rectify this without denying the importance and vitality of literature to these movements. I think of this book as a supplement to these works, not a reply.

My attention here is more structural than anything. I am mainly interested in understanding why the moments when literature is in close proximity to resistance movements are so fleeting and also, more recently, so rare. A condition that is all the more interesting because it is a moment where the writing of literature is often presumed to be a form of activism. However, I do not rigorously define resistance movements and this should not be mistaken for a study of these movements. I understand resistance as a series of ever-evolving social formations, formations that are antagonistic in some way to some part of the nation-state. I do not debate the successes or the contradictions of the philosophies of these movements. I do not evaluate whether their antagonism is justified or not. Nor do I quantify their reach, count their membership numbers, or make any sort of determination of their successes or failures.

I focus on three examples in this book: turn of the twentieth century avant garde modernism, movement literatures of the 1960s and 1970s, and this literature in English that includes other languages at the turn of the twenty-first century. These literatures exist because there are writers who want to fulfill Lorde's claim that poetry "forms the quality of the light within which we predicate our hopes and dreams toward survival and change, first made into language, then into idea, then into more tangible action."[40] But, as I will document in detail, each of these literatures despite their utopian and revolutionary hopes atrophy into something that makes good Adorno's claim that "this is not a time for political works of art."[41] This book is an attempt to understand that slide from Lorde to Adorno, to understand why it so persistently goes in the Lorde-to-Adorno direction and not the reverse, despite the best intentions and desires of numerous writers and readers of engaged work.

Some of this slide is the result of literature's complicated relationship to capitalism. There is much about literary production that escapes the pressures of the marketplace, even though, as Anderson noticed, the book is the "first modern-style mass-produced industrial commodity."[42] Marx, of course, knew this. Milton, he famously claimed, "produced *Paradise Lost* in the way that a silkworm produces silk, as the expression of *his own* nature."[43] The silk in Marx's formulation is what writers of the sort of literature I study here, literature that is recognized as Literature in that it could be included on a syllabus or in a scholarly article, tend to celebrate as autonomy. This literature in particular (unlike genre fiction, which is often presumed to have a close relationship to the market) is authorized less from its relation to the market and more from how the silk part does not have a relation to the market. Dave Beech, in *Art and Value,* a study of art's economic exceptionalism, calls this relationship "art's anomalous, incomplete and paradoxical commodification," and this, he continues, means that art is brought into capitalism as something independent from capitalism.[44] Understanding this, he adds, is crucial for understanding the "basis of art's political engagement with society."[45] This complicated half-in and half-out relationship with capitalism is what gives literature the autonomy to provoke, to speak truths to power. But it also makes it vulnerable to other sorts of conscription. The market, in short, is not the only force that might conscript literary autonomy.

Basically, the complicated relationship that literature has to capitalism means it can be instrumentalized in all sorts of ways. Some of these ways matter to me. Autonomy from market pressures was part of the reason that literature could be such an important form for culturalist movements in the late 1960s and 1970s. But in the contemporary moment it is what has forced literature into a dependency on various governmental institutions.

I often use the word "autonomy" in this book. I use it bluntly (and a bit like Casanova does). A literature is autonomous when it is free from outside interference, from the market, from the government. Writers do not have autonomy if their work is obstructed by their own government, whether that obstruction take the form of censorship or the form of amplifying certain work over others while acting as if what Casanova calls the world republic of letters is a level playing field. When literature is instrumentalized by the government as the good form of protest and then used to suppress more militant dissent, it is not autonomous. I am, in short, using the word "autonomy" in a much more simplistic way than, as Andrew Goldstone points out in *Fictions of Autonomy,* it has been used historically.[46] I do not consider the moments when writers decide to align their work with various political movements a restriction on autonomy. (I do not, thus, presume that "autonomy" means freedom from politics even though it is often used to mean this.) As I worked on this book, I became more and more of an absolutist when it comes to autonomy. It is, I have come to realize, something I value, even as I get that it is obviously impossible to have a totally autonomous literature, that literature always has commercial pressures, whether they come from the market or from patrons, that literature is so integral to nationalism that it almost always has some form of governmental support.

This book is written, after this introduction, in four sections. I begin in the first section by discussing this literature of the turn of the twenty-first century that I see as attempting to be "revolutionary" in its language use. My argument is that these writers were doing what many writers do, attempting to not only be autonomous, in a Casanova way, but also to be resistant. And they were doing it in the ways that many writers before them had done it: through separating themselves from the language conventions of the state. In this chapter, I list about thirty writers from various locales who wrote works in English that included other languages at the turn of the twenty-first century; these works include over thirty languages, among them Aymara, Arabic, Dutch, Faroese, Filipino, Fon, French, German, Gilbertese, Greek, Guarani, Hawaiian, Hebrew, Hungarian, Italian, Korean, Latin, Maori, Narragansett, Nhautl, Pidgin, Polish, Portuguese, Quechua, Romanian, Sanskrit, Shona, Spanish, Twi, West African Patois, and Yoruba. My listing though is obviously far from complete.

The term that I use for this literature—"literature in English that includes other languages"—is undeniably unwieldy. I have tried repeatedly to edit it out, to turn it into an acronym, to avoid it. I have given up. One reason I insist on such an unwieldy phrase is that I want to mark that I am talking about a literature written in English, even as this literature includes other languages. This literature is unevenly bilingual, often so uneven that it does not even deserve the qualification of "bi-." Much of this literature presumes that readers will have fluency in English but not necessarily in the other languages. Much of it uses English syntaxes and tends to include words or phrases in other languages. Sometimes, although less often, a sentence will be in another language. It is rare, though, to see a paragraph written completely in another language. These are also works published by English-language presses and distributed through English-language networks. Their ancillary material, such as their jacket copy and copyright page, is in English.

I have also kept this unwieldy term because I am talking about a sort of literature that is both more specific and larger than what scholars such as Marc Shell and Werner Sollors collect in their *Multilingual Anthology of American Literature,* an anthology written entirely in languages other than English, and also than what scholars such as Mary Louise Pratt, Doris Sommer, and others define as "bilingual."[47] It is more specific in that I am talking about a literature written in English for English language readers. It is larger in that I am talking about the "bilingual" traditions that so define the literature of the U.S.-Mexico border while talking about a poet such as Kim who brings her heritage language into her work, as do many writers associated with multiculturalism, such as Anne Tardos who includes Hungarian, German, and French. While much of the borderland literature presents a knowing bilingual narrator or author, one with a heritage claim to Spanish or English, I am also interested in works where mainly English writers include languages that they do not claim as a part of their heritage or include languages that they do not claim to know with a learned fluency so the narrator cannot be the knowing bilingual of Sommer's work.

My argument in this first chapter relies not only on Casanova's work. I have learned much from various studies of dialect or vernacular literatures in the United States such as Gavin Jones's *Strange Talk,* Michael North's *The Dialect of Modernism,* and Bryan Wagner's *Disturbing the Peace* even as the works that I discuss are not written in dialect (with one exception: in the third chapter I discuss the trouble that is John Barr's *Grace*). While dialect writing in the nineteenth century was often used, as Jones argues, for "certain types of political criticism, especially among those who were alienated from centers of power, by creating another level of discourse in which deep ethical convictions could be safely represented," one of my presumptions is that dialect writing is somewhat suspect by the turn of the twenty-first century.[48] Most obviously, its attention to regional concerns is not that relevant to writers at the turn of the century who are wrestling with globalization. This might also explain why there are at the turn of the twenty-first century several epic poems set in an imagined future that are written in globalized idiolects such as Cathy Park Hong's *Dance Dance Revolution* (written in a mixture of English, Korean, Latin, and Spanish) and Øyvind Rimbereid's *Solaris korrigert* (written in a mixture of Norwegian dialects, English, Danish, German, and Dutch). Wagner documents another hesitation: the complicated way that nineteenth-century vernacular cultural production parallels the rise of police power and is used "to stage continuously its inevitability before the public."[49] Yet at the same time, the work done by scholars who are attentive to some of the complications around dialect writing usefully shaped my work. When Jones writes that "dialect could encode the possibility of resistance, not just by undermining the integrity of a dominant standard, but by recording the subversive voices in which alternate versions of reality were engendered," his noticing applies equally to this literature written in English that includes other languages.[50] That dialect connotes a different possibility in the nineteenth century than it does at the turn of the twenty-first century is a sign of how important it is to remember that the political valences of literary forms are provisional, contextual, and always evolving.

Then in two related chapters grouped under the title "Stubborn Nationalism," I tell a transcontinental history of the troubled relationship between literature and the nation-state after World War II. I concentrate mainly on the United States, on the CIA's use of literature as cultural diplomacy, on the FBI's harassment of movement literatures in the 1960s and 1970s, and on the alliances between these U.S. governmental agencies and private foundations such as the Ford and Rockefeller. To tell this story, I focus on the specific yet related histories of avant garde modernism, anticolonial literatures of the mid-century, and movement literatures of the 1960s and 1970s.

"Example One, Avant Garde Modernism" begins with Gertrude Stein. I use her work as an example of how complicated and counterintuitive this relationship between literature and the state can be. I first examine how Stein's work fits Casanova's reading of modernist literature as other than national because of its atypical language use. Paying special attention to how Stein's work was presented in Eugene Jolas's little magazine *Transition*, I argue for a reading of avant garde modernism that acknowledges how its aesthetics are under the influence of the sweeping changes to culture that are the result of colonialism. I argue that avant garde modernism was an attempt by many writers to write a literature that was autonomous and resistant. I also discuss how

Stein's work was easily recuperated into U.S. post–World War II Cold War concerns and use as an example her linguistically atypical play *Four Saints in Three Acts,* which was produced in Europe by the Congress for Cultural Freedom as a tool of cultural diplomacy. From there, I tell the story of the development of Cold War cultural diplomacy with special attention to the large number of little magazines that the CIA either started or infiltrated during the 1950s and 1960s. As I do this, I trace how U.S. cultural diplomacy concerns morph from an anticommunism to an anticolonialism (which is still an anticommunism) after the Bandung Conference and the somewhat related Congress of Black Writers and Artists held by the journal *Présence Africaine.* And I point out that as the literatures that come out of African decolonization movements have a fairly significant impact on U.S. movement literatures of the 1960s and 1970s, to understand the potential autonomy of midcentury U.S. literatures one has to also understand that the idea that there should be in Africa a form of English-language literary production that is recognizable in the West as literature is something that the CIA controlled on multiple fronts.

"Example Two, Movement Literatures" moves from the CIA and focuses on both the harassment and the recuperation of movement literature by the FBI, with the help of private foundations, in the late 1960s and early 1970s. Here I first chart the development of a resistant literature with ties to political movements. The relation between political movements and movement literature of the late 1960s and early 1970s is often fairly direct. I notice the concerns with revolutionary culture and with community-controlled distribution and publication in this section in two exemplary works: Rodolfo "Corky" Gonzales's *I Am Joaquin* and Gwendolyn Brooks's *Riot.* Then I point out that the moment that produced these two works is brief and fleeting. And in the last half of this section, I locate this short life as the result of FBI harassment that mainly took the form of a harassing-implied monitoring of writers associated with these movements and, at moments, took more extreme forms. The Watts Writers Workshop was firebombed, for instance, by an FBI informant. I also in this section try to understand the impact of recuperative funding from private foundations such as the moment when the Ford Foundation in direct response to the hot summers of the 1960s and 1970s put $100 million into various militancy-quelling projects. I end the chapter by discussing the impact of the institutionalization of culturalist movements and of creative writing in higher education.

These two chapters, as they cover a lot of geographic ground and have a large historical scope, rely on much previous scholarship. I draw from Brent Hayes Edwards's and Tyler Stovall's attention to the unique impact that colonialism had on the cultural production that was happening in Paris. I discuss Greg Barnhisel's, Andrew Rubin's, Frances Stoner Saunders's, and Joel Whitney's work on the impact of the Cold War on national cultures. I rely on William Maxwell's attention to the FBI's harassment of black writers and from CIA and FBI files as well as diplomatic cables. I add to this the various studies of how private foundations worked with the State Department to quell midcentury dissent by Noliwe Rooks, Fabio Rojas, Karen Ferguson, and Jodi Melamed. And I also build on Mark McGurl's and Eric Bennett's attention to the relationship between higher education and creative writing. I have in this book attempted to gather these splintered histories together to better understand how they work in concert with each other. What I add to this work is an attention to how these forces multiply and amplify each other as the century goes on. Most studies that document the synergies between the state and private foundations, for instance, tend to see these synergies in isolation.

From there, I return in the fourth chapter to the turn of the twenty-first century so as to understand the continuing resonances of these forces. As Evan Kindley notes in *Poet-Critics and the Administration of Culture,* "Much of what we view as our robust vernacular culture of poetic composition and instruction could easily be decimated with a stroke of an administrator's pen or a change in priorities on the part of a foundation officer."[51] Here I trace the ongoing and intensifying synergy between higher education, the state, and private foundations through the State Department's use of literature as a crucial component of cultural diplomacy after 9/11, the Bush administration's funding of the National Endowment for the Arts and Dana Gioia's oversight of these funds, the rise of what Steve Evans calls "Poets for Bush," the inaugural poems of the Clinton and Obama administrations, and the use of state-sponsored multiculturalism as a tool of cultural diplomacy. As I point out, one of the many peculiarities of literary culture at the end of the century is that literary activism is often presumed to be synonymous with institutionalization.

A brief conclusion ponders whether things can be otherwise. I answer more or less no, or not in any way that I can yet see.

My scholarly debts in this story are huge and various. I have thought of this study as primarily a post-postcolonial one, even while it is a study of the literatures of empire. But one of my presumptions is that it is difficult to understand what is happening to literature at the turn of the twenty-first century without the attention that postcolonialism gave to literature's relation to the colonial nation-state, both how imperial literatures are often used as a tool to extend colonialism and, in opposition, how literature can be a crucial part of indigenous nationalism's resistance to the colonial nation-state. This is true even though, as Subramanian Shankar points out in *Flesh and Fish Blood,* postcolonial studies has in the aggregate focused most of its attention on English-language works without much thought about what it might mean to have a postcolonial canon so dependent on a literature written in a colonial and imposed language. This has meant that post-colonial scholarship has not spent much time on the importance of what he calls "vernacular knowledges": "those orientated away from the transnational, the modern, and the hybrid and toward the local, the traditional, and the culturally autonomous."[52] This study, because it is a study of literature written in English, does not counter his concerns but it does attempt to learn from them. Similarly, more sociological studies of the book, especially Sarah Brouillette's and Gauri Viswanathan's work, have helped me to understand the relation of literature to imperialism. I have thought of this study as in part allied to much of the current work that Brouillette is doing in a more global context on the impact that trends in governmental "cultural policy" have on literary pro-duction. This book is also influenced in all sorts of obvious ways by more sociological attentions to literary culture. References to Franco Moretti's work have more or less fallen out of various revisions, but his attention to how forms and genres cluster in *Graphs, Maps, and Trees* is what allowed me to notice this cluster of works that are written in English and include other languages at the turn of the twenty-first century.

There are also a number of things that conventionally get said about language and its relation to literature and individual sub-jectivity that I do not address in this study. Although I am con-vinced the answer is more or less a firm no, I skip much of the debate about whether there can be a meaningful "native" speaker of any language. I do not, for instance, spend much time with Jacques Derrida's "logical contradiction," his claim that "I only have one language; it is not mine."[53] Nor do I explore some of the similar complications that define Rey Chow's *Not Like a Native Speaker: On Languaging as a Postcolonial Experience.*[54] At the same time, I avoid moral or ethical appeals for language preservation, even while I do believe that languages can hold specific, local information in them and that language loss risks losing this localized information. But languages have always come and gone and splintered and evolved. And what is an expansionist and imposed language in one era frequently fractures and morphs into various new languages in the next era. Languages often transform from being imposed to being native over time. It cannot be otherwise. And yet none of this counters that languages are in any one moment loaded with histories, both personal ones and cultural ones. And writers, especially anticolonial writers, engage with and react to these histories. Obviously, the importance that writers who are part of decolonization struggles in the twentieth century gave to language shapes the aesthetics of their work and this in turn shapes the aesthetics of turn of the twenty-first century literatures in English.

Despite my insistence that it is impossible to understand anything about literature without seeing it as in a relation to nationalism, I do not want to suggest in any way that literature is best understood through national categories. This study is transnational even as it insists on the continuing importance of the nation-state to literary production. Here I might echo Matthew Hart and Jim Hansen who rightly insist that the state "has been forced into new relations with a variety of local and global actors, to be sure; it even comes in nonnational garb. But whatever its appearance, the state and its agents have not left the scene. Contemporary literary production surely involves the crossing and confounding of national borders—if not in practice, then in imagination. But those borders—in practice, if not in imagination—are also policed by states with access to ever more panoptical forms of protection and control."[55]

Finally, and I want to state this very clearly, this study is about how literary production is shaped by forces external to it. I am interested in the result of this long history of governmental meddling in literary production and the impact it has on contemporary literature. Because I learned so much that I know about literature from higher education (and I am not alone in this), what I learned is a State Department version of what matters. This study is an attempt to understand that. I do not believe that writers could refuse these structures away. This study does not presume that there are good writers who avoided these structures and bad ones that did not. Nor do I believe that when writers or editors take this money that they instantly lose the autonomy of their thought and become propaganda puppets. What writers do within these structures varies widely. This is also not a study built around the idea that money corrupts; that literature should or ever could be free of the market or the grant system or even higher education. I am not against funding for the arts. I am instead noticing how it skews. And if I have any lament it is that there is no robust counter. There is no moment where a significant amount of funding for the arts was awarded by any sort of organization with a politics that is anything more contestatory than liberal. It is almost impossible to imagine what it would be like if something like the Anarchist Black Cross Federation or Cooperation Jackson had millions to give out to artists. Impossible to imagine politically and impossible to imagine what this literature might look like, what forms it might take, what languages it might use. I have often thought of this as a moment when the relationship between literature and resistance is somewhat analogous to the earth's ailing ecosystem, at risk because of multiple forces that mutually reinforce each other in ways that are expansive and self-reinforcing. And while I am not so naïve as to believe that if we got rid of government and foundation manipulation of culture that it would be an egalitarian field of production and everyone would enter it as equals, I do think that the fact that cultural autonomy is impossible is not a reason to avoid attempting to understand some of the more obvious ways that it gets restricted and the long-term consequences of this.

CHAPTER ONE

Turn of the Twenty-First Century

A Possible Literature of Resistance

⌘

A PROVOCATION: in a move every bit as revolutionary as Dante's decision to write in the vernacular, at the turn of the twenty-first century more and more writers of English-language literature begin to include languages other than English in their work. I say a provocation because the writers who do this are not members of a school. They are aesthetically, geographically, and culturally unrelated. They do not announce their arrival with manifestos. Nor do they edit themselves together into anthologies. And there is scant scholarship that recognizes their similarities and theorizes why this happens.

But one likely explanation for this increase in English-language works that include other languages is that the English language was unusually contested at the turn of the twenty-first century. By the end of the twentieth century, English was the dominant or official language in over sixty countries and was represented in every continent and on three major oceans.

And it was continuing to grow. After colonialism, the growth and dominance of English was (and continues to be) primarily driven by economics, by international trade's need for a lingua franca. Yet at the same time, English was (and continues to be), as Alastair Pennycock notices, "a direct threat to the very existence of other languages. More generally, however, if not actually threatening linguistic genocide, it poses the less dramatic but far more widespread danger of what we might call linguistic curtailment. When English becomes the first choice as a second language, when it is the language in which so much is written and in which so much of the visual media occur, it is constantly pushing other languages out of the way, curtailing their usage in both qualitative and quantitative terms."[1] It was often said at the time that a language died every two weeks (because of globalization). The source of this claim is not known, but David Crystal repeats it in his book *Language Death* and it shows up again and again in articles in the *New York Times, LA Times, National Geographic,* and so on.[2] More recent work from the Endangered Languages Project estimates that one language dies every four months, a number that the project claims has been consistent for the last forty years.[3] But no matter the actual numbers, there was at the turn of the twenty-first century a significant amount of both popular and scholarly attention paid to linguicide.[4] Many scholars began research projects to catalogue dying languages. Various language revitalization and preservation projects were begun. Within the United States, the government even began to offer some protection to Native American languages through the Native American Languages Act of 1990, which declared it a U.S. federal policy to preserve, protect, and promote the rights and freedoms of Native Americans to use, practice, and develop Native American languages. In 1993 the United Nations proclaimed a

Year of Indigenous Peoples and the its Draft Declaration of the Rights of Indigenous Peoples included language in their statement of support for the rights of indigenous people to practice and revitalize their cultural traditions and customs. In Hawai'i attention to the Hawaiian language increased. The Department of Education established Pūnana Leo (Hawaiian-language preschools) and Hawaiian-immersion K–12 classrooms.

English arrived in North America fairly recently (after the term "America" arrived). In other words, it is a colonial and imposed language. More than 169 languages are indigenous to the United States and about 430 languages are spoken there.[5] And again, similar to the localism that comes with globalism, the growth in English and the economic and technological centrality of the United States means that at the end of the 1990s, as more and more words were also spoken in English in places new to English, more and more words that were not a part of English were being spoken within the country. Immigration rose dramatically in the United States in the 1990s. Foreign-born residents were at a low of 4.7 percent in 1970.[6] By 2013, foreign-born residents made up more than 13 percent of the U.S. population (below the previous high of 14.8 percent that was last seen in the 1890s).[7] The number of U.S. residents who declare that they spoke a language other than English at home has steadily risen with those numbers. In 1990, that number was over 31 million. By 2000, it was close to 47 million.[8] And by 2011, it was over 60 million.[9]

Still, even though the U.S. government does not have an "official" language, the collection of words and syntaxes that is called "English" has an unchallenged dominance within the United States and the country's consistent underfunding of language acquisition programs in its schools makes it unlikely that this will change any time soon. In some parts of the United States,

English's dominance is maintained by institutional fiat, such as in Hawai'i, where if it were not for the Department of Education's legislative restrictions, Pidgin (also called Hawai'i Creole English by linguists) might thrive and even dominate. Claude Hagège calls this a war and reminds how recently English became the language of composition in the Pacific: "the war that the United States waged during the first decades of the twentieth century on the languages spoken on the various islands of Micronesia, like Chamorro (or Guameño) on Guam, as well as other languages on Saipan, Rota, Tinian, Pagan, Anatahan, and Alamagan. American power, even more than Spanish power before it, did its best to annihilate Chamorro through very strict administrative measures, and achieved a spectacular reduction in the number of its speakers."[10]

Basically, the relationship between English and the state was unusually clear during this time. So clear that despite English's assured status as the de facto language of the United States and despite English becoming more and more dominant in a world arena, there paradoxically arose at the end of the century various groups of people within the United States who worried that English was at risk and attempted to pass legislation to make English the "official" language.[11] This anxiety can probably be attributed to the increase in immigration and number of U.S. citizens who speak languages other than English in the home. And xenophobia is, of course, a tool often used by the politicians of nation-states. These "English only" and "English plus" lobbying groups received a huge amount of media attention in the late 1980s and into the 1990s and had some limited success. ("English plus" is often presented to voters as a less reactionary alternative to "English only" legislation because it supposedly acknowledges the presence of languages other than English, but it more or less has the same effect as "English only" as it legalizes English as a dominant language.) Before 1987, seven states had some sort of legislation that privileged English: California (1986), Illinois (1969), Indiana (1984), Kentucky (1984), Massachusetts (1975), Nebraska (1920), and Tennessee (1984). It is worth noting that prior to 1984, only three states were concerned enough about language issues to have English-only legislation. (Hawai'i is an interesting exception: various occupying governments outlawed Hawaiian in the 1890s and it was made an official state language in the 1970s.) By 1990, another ten had joined the trend: in 1987, Arkansas, Mississippi, North Carolina, North Dakota, and South Carolina made English the official and only language of the government. In 1988, Colorado and Florida followed suit; in 1989 New Mexico, Oregon, and Washington passed "English plus" resolutions; and in 1990, Alabama passed legislation to make English the official and only language of the government. In 1992, Rhode Island passed an "English plus" resolution. In 1995, Alabama, Montana, New Hampshire, and South Dakota passed legislation to make English the official and only language of the government. There was also the 1996 controversy around the Oakland school board's discussion about whether to institutionally recognize that many of their students spoke Ebonics, or what linguists tend to call "African American Vernacular English" (a controversy manufactured mainly by a conservative media). From 1996 to 2006, Georgia, Virginia, Wyoming, Missouri, Utah, Iowa, and Arizona passed legislation to make English the official and only language of the government. Currently twenty-six states have some sort of Official English legislation (thirty if you count "English plus"). What all this legislation means finally is not much more than a statement of support for racism and xenophobia since most of these states still have to produce government documents in other languages.

What I am trying to describe here is how at the turn of the century, the English language was a site of attention, a vexed one defined by contradictions. It was expanding globally. While remaining firmly entrenched in the United States, it was more and more frequently forced to coexist with other languages because of an increase in the use of languages other than English. And there was, as a result, a rise in language-focused xenophobia. At the same time, globally, a large number of languages were disappearing at an alarming rate. Basically, language, the very material of composition for literature, received a huge amount of attention at the end of the century. But not just any language and not just any attention. The attention focused on English and its role as both the language of imperial and economic globalization and of U.S. nationalism. The English language at this moment was in short in no way a language of liberation and for many it was a language of oppression. As a result, much English-language literature of the time reflects and comments on this very intense public debate about language that was also a discussion about imperialism and about indigenous and immigrant rights. These discussions changed not only literature in English, but also governing bodies and public school systems. This alone means that merely to include another language in one's work, any other language, was a pointed statement for these writers (although the sort of pointing that it does of course varies from writer to writer). And similarly, to write a realist novel in Standard English was also a pointed statement.

As the writers in English who include other languages in their work are not aligned, there is some variance in intent and in the languages included. Many writers bring heritage languages into their work. Anne Tardos's *Uxudo,* for example, moves relentlessly between Hungarian, German, French, and English, languages that Tardos learned in a childhood spent with French resistance parents who were constantly moving to avoid anti-Semitism.[12] Mark Nowak in *Revenants*—an exploration of the Polish American communities of his childhood around Buffalo, New York— uses Polish, a language that has little state support in the United States, is rarely taught in schools, and yet has a fairly significant presence there.[13] Judy Halebsky's *Space/Gap/Interval/Distance* is full of Japanese kanji.[14] Padcha Tuntha-obas's *Trespasses* moves from English and into Thai.[15]

And those who were writing in dialogue with traditions that were already bi- or multilingual often intensified this gesture at the turn of the century. Chicano/a and Nuyorican literatures were more bilingual (and often trilingual) than not in the late 1960s and early 1970s, particularly Chicano/a literature. Many foundational works, such as Rodolfo "Corky" Gonzales's *I Am Joaquin,* Alurista's *Nationchild Plumaroja, 1969–1972,* and Juan Felipe Herrera's *Rebozos of Love/We Have Woven/Sudor de Pueblos/On Our Back,* move easily between English and Spanish.[16] But by the turn of the century, the literature that came out of these traditions was less enthusiastic about Spanish as a language of liberation. Edwin Torres, for instance, as many a Nuyorican writer before him, liberally included Spanish in his English-language works. But his work repeatedly questions the untroubled representation of Spanish as the "correct" marker of identity for anyone in the Americas, tearing both languages apart as he stutters between languages about the impossibility of language being constitutive of identity: "I yo NEO-why KNOW who say NO you say ME I see WHY Know NUYO know YOU."[17] Hugo García Manríquez's *Anti-Humboldt: A Reading of the North American*

Free Trade Agreement, written half in English and half in Spanish, presents both English and Spanish as languages of the state, not of identity.[18] Francisco X. Alarcón in *Snake Poems* brings not just Spanish (a heritage language for him) but also Nahuatl into his English. In these short, lyrical poems he repeatedly returns to the phrase "I myself," to a statement of identity that he puts in dialogue with the Nahuatl phrase "nomatca nehuatl," not with the Spanish.[19] Related but different: Cecilia Vicuña in *Unraveling Words and the Weaving of Water,* a collection of translated works that have Spanish as their primary language of composition, moves through various languages: Spanish, Sanskrit, Nahuatl, Latin, German, Greek, Guarani, Quechua, and Aymara.[20]

A similar story of linguistic intensification can be told about literature written in Pidgin in Hawai'i. The first literary book in Pidgin might be 1972's *Chalukyu Eensai* by Bradajo (Jozuf Hadley).[21] Darrell H. Y. Lum's first fiction collection in Pidgin, *Sun: Short Stories and Drama* was published in 1980.[22] But for the most part, in the 1970s and into the 1980s, if Pidgin showed up, it tended to show up as accent or local color in works with a standard English omniscient voice. Then, in the 1990s, various local presses such as Bamboo Ridge and Tinfish published a number of books in which Pidgin was a compositional language for entire poems, sometimes even entire books such as Eric Chock's *Last Days Here,* Lois-Ann Yamanaka's *Saturday Night at the Pahala Theatre,* Lee Tonouchi's *Da Word,* Kathy Dee Kaleokealoha Kaloloahilani Banggo's *4-evaz, Anna,* and Lisa Linn Kanae's *Sista Tongue.*[23] And by the mid-1990s in Hawai'i, there might have been as much literature written in Pidgin as in English.

Even more distinctive to this period was the large number of writers who brought in languages that were indigenous, that did not travel, or that were not a part of colonialism. Sometimes these languages were not part of the author's cultural heritage. Rosmarie Waldrop is a writer whose career spans decades and who writes mainly in Standard English. In the 1990s she published *A Key into the Language of America,* a work that uses a series of Narragansett phrases taken from Roger Williams's book of the same name (Waldrop has no fluency in Narragansett). More commonly, however, writers turn to indigenous languages that are part of their cultural heritage. Diane Glancy's early work reflects the generic and yet localized specificity of much free verse lyric written at the time but more and more native languages show up in her work in the 1990s, such as *Lone Dogs Winter Count* (see especially "Death Cry for the Language") and *The Voice That Was in Travel.*[24] Guillermo Gómez-Peña's *Warrior for Gringostroika* uses Spanish and Nahuatl.[25] Robert Sullivan uses Maori in *Star Waka.*[26] James Thomas Stevens and Caroline Sinavaiana wrote *Mohawk/Samoa: Transmigration* together, a work that includes Mohawk (written by Stevens) and Samoan (written by Sinavaiana) songs next to each other, each song first in its original language, then an English translation of the song, then each of them rewrite each song.[27] Stevens's other works are also focused on language. His first book, *Tōkinish,* a lyrical, personal exploration of a relationship inflected by colonial histories includes Narragansett (phrases that he, like Waldrop, took from Williams).[28] *Bulle/Chimére* opens with invocations to a beloved in Mohawk ("a T. Sgro [Sekoreh Skeen'son]") and French ("Que jamais la bulle n'élate").[29] Haunani-Kay Trask—in 1994's *Light in a Crevice Never Seen* and in 2002's *Night is a Sharkskin Drum*—writes a distinctly anticolonial poetry in an English that liberally includes Hawaiian.[30] Alani Apio's *Kāmau* and *Kāmau A'e,* the first two plays of a trilogy (the third play has been produced but not published), use English, Hawaiian, and Pidgin.[31] Teresia Kieuea

Teaiwa uses English and Gilbertese in parts of *Searching for Nei Nim'anoa*.[32] Kristin Naca's *Bird Eating Bird* has poems in English and Spanish and her poem titles are in Tagalog.[33] Craig Santos Perez's trilogy, three books that he gathered under the title *From Unincorporated Territory*, registers the globalism of Guam brought on by colonialism through the inclusion of the languages of Chamoru, Spanish, and Japanese.

Other writers deliberately include colonial languages, often in works that are about colonialism. M. NourbeSe Philip writes one of the more interesting examples of this in *She Tries Her Tongue: Her Silence Softly Breaks*.[34] In "Universal Grammar," Philip takes a single clichéd sentence about a tall, blond, blue-eyed, white-skinned man and moves it through Portuguese, Spanish, Dutch, French, German, and English, the languages of nineteenth-century colonialism. Her most recent book *Zong!*, about the slave ship of the same name and slavery's legacy, moves through fourteen different languages: Arabic, Dutch, Fon, French, Greek, Hebrew, Italian, Latin, Portuguese, Spanish, Shona, Twi, West African Patois, and Yoruba.[35] Walter Lew in *Excerpts from: ∆ikth / 딕테/ 딕티/DIKTE for DICTEE* (1982), a book that is about Theresa Hak Kyung Cha's *DICTEE* (a book that was first published in 1982, but does not really enter any canon—either Asian American or "experimental"—until the 1990s), echoes the globalized multilingualism of *DICTEE* and includes French and English with some Korean, Chinese, and Greek.[36] Cathy Park Hong's *Dance Dance Revolution* is written in a future imagined idiolect that is a combination of English, Korean, Latin, and Spanish.[37] Jonathan Stalling's *Yingelishi* combines English and Chinese.[38]

But despite these disparities, there are overlapping concerns. These works are more global than national in form for sure. But they never present globalization as something distinct from the national and usually are trying to understand the impact of globalization, not just on cultural production but also on their own lives. Kim writes of the language juxtapositions she uses to write *Commons* as setting in "concurrent motion, these texts were 'translated' simultaneously. It is not the actual translation or even the state of translatability between the two texts that is intriguing but the possibilities for transcribing what occurs in the transversal between the two languages (and, by extension, between the two 'nations,' their mutually implicated histories of colonization, political conflicts, and so on)."[39] These books often turn their attention to trade routes. Kim is an obvious example here too. Chris Chen notices this when he calls *Dura* "an exploration of what cultural meaning can be made out of the reticular networks of labor and exchange ceaselessly bringing populations together and splitting them apart."[40] *Dura* and *Commons* both tell a story about capital's distributions. *Dura* calls forth "Globe and a model of the planet" and also "Proof: 1492, the first terrestrial globe."[41] The section "Measure" goes to the ships, "Ships of trade accompanied by ships of war," to "(Capital)" and "To speak of another region and its goods."[42] There is a moment in *Dura* where Kim writes "Translate: 38th parallel. Translate: the first shipload of African slaves was landed at Jamestown."[43] The 38th Parallel, the line that separates North and South Korea, is also the line that crosses the San Francisco Bay (the line on which Kim was living in California when she wrote *Dura)* and the line that crosses the continent to include the Chesapeake Bay and Jamestown. The 38th Parallel, as it is a middle latitude without dramatic climate extremes, has long had major civilizations located along it. The spatiality here is connected globally, fully historical, and attentive to U.S. nationalism as a form of imperialism: Jamestown, the first permanent English settlement on the continent; the 38th

Parallel that divides North and South Korea created by the United States at the Potsdam Conference. When Kim demands that we translate the 38th Parallel she does not mean to move from one language to the other and in the process make literature monolingual or easily decipherable. Her concern is for something more investigative, more suggestive, for something like the 38th Parallel of her personal narrative to be understood as a larger historical narrative, as the result of globalizing capitalism.

Gómez-Peña's work returns again and again to the new geopolitical alliances that are being formed at the turn of the century. He notices that he is "a writer in Mexico, where writers are respected and heard, and a performance artist in the United States, where writers are marginalized."[44] And the maps that his works make are the maps that NAFTA formalized in 1994. In "The Border Is . . . (A Manifesto)" he notes "a new cartography; a brand-new map to host the new project; the democratization of the East; the socialization of the West; the Third-Worldization of the North and First-Worldization of the South."[45]

These works are also full of language lessons and bureaucratic questions about language. For instance, Stevens's "Alphabet of Letters" in *A Bridge Dead in the Water* "explores the propaganda found in Native American children's primers from the time of our honored Mohawk chief, Joseph Brant, and the propaganda of rhetoric in general."[46] Vicuña's work is full of idiosyncratic definitions and etymologies, the point of which seems to be to suggest a sort of connected linguistic culture. As she writes in *Instan,* "A word is a non-place for the encounter to take 'place.' / A continuous displacement, a field of 'con,' togetherness. / A word disappears, the connection remains."[47]

Again, Kim's work is full of examples. In *Under Flag* she asks "Can you read and write English? Yes _____. No _____."[48] In

The Bounty, the poem "Primer" announces "This is the study book" as an epigraph and charts comparisons between Korean to English:

mostly translations of	inculcate its shame	to learn
the Scriptures into Chinese		the English
which educated Koreans		of a Midwest town
could read[49]		

In "Thirty and Five Books" in *Dura:* "9.8 One of the first words understood in English: stupid."[50] Also in *Dura,* "Cosmography" includes a section that looks like the short answer part of a language quiz, the definitions are in English and the answers that fill in the blank are in Hangul. "Hummingbird" also begins with what looks like a quiz, a somewhat difficult and impossible to imagine quiz but still one that begins with the request for a name.

And so many examples from the Pacific. Each of Trask's books ends with a glossary that, as Anderson notes about early indigenous language dictionaries, functions as a sort of "how-to" of political resistance.[51] The glossary at the back of *Night Is a Sharkskin Drum,* for instance, goes like this:

'āina	Land, earth
'āina aloha	Beloved land
'āina hānau	The land of one's birth[52]

Teaiwa's *Searching for Nei Nim'anoa* also has a somewhat idiosyncratic glossary at the back of the book, one that has a section called "Loose interpretations of broken Gilbertese" and another of "U.S.-specific references" that jokingly explains terms like "ATM" and also telephone companies and banks: "AT&T,"

"MCI," "SPRINT," and "Wells Fargo."[53] Kanae's *Sista Tongue* uses a story about Kanae's brother learning to talk and in the process ruminates about what it means to speak Pidgin in Hawai'i, a language that she presents as resistant. Tonouchi's story "pijin wawrz," included in his collection *Da Word*, is a parodic response to some of the debates about how to write in Pidgin that were happening in Hawai'i in the 1990s. The story features a mechanical being named "Big Ben" (after Governor Ben Cayatano) who bans Pidgin and "Da Pidgin Guerilla æn hiz armi awv rebolz."[54] Tonouchi writes the narrative frame in Odo Orthography (a phonemic transcription system for Pidgin developed by linguists Derek Bickerton and Carol Odo in the 1970s) and he writes the character's speech in literary Pidgin. Using Odo Orthography is a bit of a joke on the discussions that surround how to write Pidgin as it is very hard to read for many who easily read literary Pidgin. Yamanaka's "Tita: Boyfriends" has a moment where one teenage girl literally schools another teenage girl about language when she talks about how she exaggerates her Standard English when wanting to seduce a boy:

> Richard wen' call me around 9:05 last night
> Nah, I talk real nice to him.
> Tink I talk to him the way I talk to you?
> You cannot let boys know your true self.
> Here, this how I talk.
> Hello, Richard. How are you?[55]

While I realize that the literature of Hawai'i is often treated as if it is peripheral to continental understandings of American literature (and even within Hawai'i many want to claim an autonomy from American literature), Hawai'i provides an unusually succinct example here of both the importance of literature to nationalism and of resistance to nationalism at the turn of the twenty-first century. As a result of its colonial occupation by the United States and the migration patterns that fed its plantation system during the sugar boom, Hawai'i has extraordinarily complex linguistic, political, and cultural situations for its writers to address. The island chain has three languages in institutionally or culturally supported daily use: English, Hawaiian, and Pidgin. Hawai'i is also one of the few places within the United States that identifies as colonized and has a thriving anticolonial movement. And cultural production of all sorts—hula, for instance, has played a particularly important role—has been a big part of this anticolonialism. Writers of or in Hawai'i face decisions about what literary traditions they will enter as they choose whether to write in any or all or some of these three languages, one with a precontact history, one colonially imposed, and one a mixture of many languages that comes out of the labor history of the plantation system.

The Hawaiian language, 'Ōlelo Hawai'i, was spoken on the islands before contact. After annexation, Hawaiian was never officially banned but it was discouraged. In 1896 Sanford B. Dole, president of the Republic of Hawai'i, signed legislation making English the official language of instruction in public and private schools. Hawaiian was then taught, if at all, as a "foreign" language. This was accompanied by pervasive cultural and economic discouragement. Hawaiian speakers thus diminished over the nineteenth century. As Noelani Arista writes, "Simply put, Hawaiian is an indigenous language, one of innumerable languages almost eradicated towards the end of the nineteenth century through complex processes of global imperialism."[56]

This began to change around the middle of the twentieth century and Hawaiian was recognized as an "official" language at the 1978 Constitutional Convention. A concerted effort to preserve and expand the use of the Hawaiian language followed. Hawaiian was used as a language of instruction at the University of Hawai'i at Hilo in 1982. Pūnana Leo (Hawaiian language preschools) were established in 1985 and Department of Education Hawaiian Immersion K–12 classrooms in 1987.[57] By 2015, over 18,000 people claimed to speak Hawaiian at home.

Pidgin, which is frequently used in informal settings, developed into a language (and not just a grammatically simplified communication that is never a first language) after 1898 when Hawaiian was banned and English became the language of instruction.[58] The Department of Education and the Boards of Education of Hawai'i attempted to ban or regulate Pidgin and continue to do so today. In 1924 an "English Standard System" was adopted that grouped K–12 students by their language proficiency in English. The system was a fairly intense form of segregation and it was in place until 1948. After the demise of English Standard, the Board of Education repeatedly discussed officially banning Pidgin in the classroom. In 1987 (interestingly the same year that the Hawai'i State Legislature passed a resolution for the Department of Education to implement classes taught in Hawaiian and the same year the Hawaiian Language Immersion Programs were established), a ban did not pass, but weaker legislation that encouraged teachers to "model" English in the classroom did.[59] There were hints that a ban might happen even as recently as 1999.[60]

Further complicating, and unlike Hawaiian, Pidgin is a language formed by colonialism, even if not in the name of colonization. And while there have been some scholarly studies about

Pidgin, and many books of literature that use Pidgin as the language of composition, it is not a language that has yet reached the status of acquirable by outsiders through institutionalized study. The only dictionaries are popular, not scholarly, and there are rarely classes that teach the grammar.[61] Its close ties to colonialism have led some to question its political valences when used as a literary language. So while Kanae writes of how "resistance is an intrinsic element of Pidgin" and also that literature written in Pidgin "criticizes and heals the inferiority complexes and self-loathing that was created by cultural elites," Trask argues in "Decolonizing Hawaiian Literature" that local writers often celebrate Pidgin and gloss over "the absence of authentic sounds and authentic voices."[62] Rodney Morales also writes of Pidgin literature's content, "Obviously, not all of the story is being told. With a few notable exceptions, we haven't heard nearly as much from, for example, those other Asians, the Filipinos, who are overrepresented in service jobs, especially in the hotel and food industries, or Native Hawaiians, who are overrepresented in Hawaiʻi's prisons."[63]

Anthologies from the late 1970s to the late 1980s such as *Anthology Hawaii* (a special issue of the journal *Seaweeds and Constructions* that was published in 1979), *Mālama: Hawaiian Land and Water* (1985), and *Hoʻomānoa: An Anthology of Contemporary Hawaiian Literature* (1989) feature work that is mainly in English with at most a sprinkling of Hawaiian words, often marked as "foreign" by the use of italics.[64] Literature engaged with Pidgin used a similar approach. There are a few titles that appeared in the 1970s and in 1978 the first Talk Story conference was held. This conference is often mentioned as the beginning of the local and Pidgin literary renaissance. Rob Wilson calls it "a catalyst to theorize and fill in the lack of literature written by and for locals."[65]

But the anthology that came out of the conference, *Talk Story: An Anthology of Hawaii's Local Writers,* did not have that much written in Pidgin and what was included was embedded in a Standard English frame.

But beginning in the 1990s, the literature written in Hawai'i was less and less likely to be written mainly in English. Hawaiian language is included in this literature more and more. Dennis Carroll, writing about "Hawai'i's 'Local' Theatre" notes in 2000 that "one of the important developments in 'local' theatre during the past three years has been the foregrounding of the verbal languages of 'local' theatre."[66] He notes not only the foregrounding of languages other than English, but also productions of entire plays in the Hawaiian language. Writing about Tammy Haili'ōpua Baker's *Kaluaiko'olau: ke kā 'e'a'e'a o nō pali kalalau* (*Kaluaiko'olau: The Hero of the Cliffs of Kalalau*) and *Māuiakamalo: ka ho'okala kupua o ka moku* (*Māuiakamalo: The Great Ancestor of Chiefs*): "Large audiences turned out for both productions, which toured the state. In a decade in which Hawaiian has reemerged as a living language for thousands of the population, this is a most significant development."[67]

As is to be expected, much has been written in Hawai'i, in English, that is about language use and what languages are colonial and what are aligned with decolonization struggles. Apio's plays, for example, tell the story of two cousins whose ancestral lands (where they live but which they do not own) have been sold to a multinational hotel chain for development. Which language is used at what point in the plays is very pointed and full of subtext. *Kāmau* (the first play) opens with offstage exchanges between characters that are in Standard English and Pidgin. Then Alika, one of the cousins who works as a tour guide, speaks Standard English to the tourists and Pidgin to the bus driver. *Kāmau*

A'e (the second play) opens with the other cousin, Michael / Kawaipono in jail (at the end of *Kāmau* he attacked two security guards trying to remove him from the ancestral lands). The play begins in Standard English, with the warden's off-stage voice stating, "Michael Kawaipono Mahekona. Nine years you've served. Mister Mahekona, stay out of prison."[68] Onstage, Michael / Kawaipono responds in Hawaiian, "Ua lawa mākou i ka pōhaku. 'Ai pōhaku."[69] These words—which translate as "Stones are enough. Eat stones."—are translated at the end of the play, but they would be recognizable to most audience members familiar with Kānaka Maoli culture (whether they know Hawaiian or not). They are the words to "Kaulana Nā Pua" (also known as "Mele 'ai Pōhaku"), a famous protest song written by Ellen Keho'ohiwaokalani Wright Prendergast in 1893 in response to the overthrow of the Kānaka Maoli monarchy by U.S. citizens (with help from the U.S. military). It means, loosely, those who are opposed to the occupation of Hawai'i will not follow it; they will eat what remains: the stones of the earth. Noenoe Silva tells in *Aloha Betrayed: Native Hawaiian Resistance to American Colonialism* how Prendergast wrote the song after the provisional government fired the members of the Royal Hawaiian Band when they refused "to sign an oath of loyalty, swearing that they would not support the queen or her government."[70] It is indicative of Apio's political intents that the play starts with a statement in Hawaiian that is both accessible to many who do not speak Hawaiian and a highly politicized statement of solidarity. After this exchange, the play flashes back to Alika visiting Michael / Kawaipono in jail and speaking to him in Pidgin. The language politics of these opening scenes are obvious: English is the language of the occupying government; Hawaiian is the language of the imprisoned, a language that will be reclaimed by Michael /

Kawaipono in prison. Alika in the play is literally a figure of negotiation between Kānaka Maoli and Western values and he speaks mainly in Pidgin, a language of mixture and mediation that while it is particular to Hawai'i is not as suggestively anticolonial.

Language politics in Apio's plays are so resonant, so defining. In *Kāmau A'e,* Michael / Kawaipono learns Hawaiian in jail. And in both plays Michael / Kawaipono and Alika frequently argue about language as they argue about the limitations of cultural preservation and occupation-based activism in the colonial situation that defines Hawai'i. As with many of the works I consider here, legibility and language preservation are in an uneasy dialogue. Apio has, after all, written a defense of indigenous language acquisition as part of anticolonial struggle in a colonial language, in English, despite the Pidgin and Hawaiian. English is clearly the language of composition and of circulation and of the work's audience. It is crucial though to read this tension as productive, not as dismissible. Casanova, when discussing the "peculiar ambiguity of the relation of literary domination and dependence" for writers in "dominated spaces," notices that "to criticize established literary forms and genres because they have been inherited from colonial culture, for instance, misses the point that literature itself, as a value common to an entire space, is not only part of the legacy of political domination but also an instrument that, once reappropriated, permits writers from literarily deprived territories to gain recognition."[71] Apio's work is a complex and lovely and obvious example of not only this sort of reappropriation to gain recognition in the larger field of literature but also, more locally, an example of how writers might counter the restrictions that colonial states impose on local languages without resorting to a return to a language that much of the intended audience might not be able to read comfortably because colonialism has limited fluency in the local language.

Another provocative example of how loaded these language issues were for writers at the turn of the century is the similarities between Alarcón's, Stevens's, and Waldrop's works. Within two years (1992–1994) of each other, Alarcón, Stevens, and Waldrop all wrote book-length lyric-influenced poems that also included appropriated passages from a seventeenth-century document written in a colonial and an indigenous language. Stevens and Waldrop included Narragansett taken from Roger Williams's *A Key into the Language of America*.[72] Alarcón included Nahuatl taken from Hernando Ruiz de Alarcón's *Treatise on the Heathen Superstitions: That Today Live among the Indians Native to This New Spain*.[73] The similarities between these books are especially intense between Waldrop and Stevens. Both wrote their books in the early 1990s. And both were somewhat associated previous to the 1990s with the scene around Brown University's graduate creative writing program. Stevens was a student and Waldrop was the spouse of Keith Waldrop, who taught at Brown. (Waldrop and Stevens both claim to not have known that the other was working with the Williams text until after they had written their own works. Stevens wrote his book after he left Providence.)

The relationship that these works and their authors have to indigeneity are uneven. Much of Stevens's work is about indigeneity. He grew up, as his bio notes state, "between three reservations, the two where his grandparents came from, Akwesasne Territory and Six Nations Reserve, and the one where they settled, the Tuscarora Nation" and the emphasis in much of his work is not only on the continued relevance of Native American cultures, but also on the flexibility, the revisionary potential, and the resilience of these cultures in a time of continuing colonization.[74]

Stevens's interest in Narragansett culture is also not entirely arbitrary. In 1992 he worked as a data collector at the Narragansett Community House, working with inner-city children on a program called Whateanuonk that was designed to counter Providence gang and drug culture.

Waldrop is known mainly as a feminist and experimental writer. She is a German immigrant who writes literature mainly in English and publishes mainly with U.S. presses. Her work is frequently lyrical, quietly elliptical, and full of collaged language. Her relationship to Native American culture is more provisional, so much so that at moments her claims about indigenous culture are without nuance. She echoes, for instance, debunked claims that Native American cultures are more patriarchal than the cultures of European immigrants ("As a woman, I have no illusions about Indian societies. They were far from ideal.").[75]

Alarcón is likewise defined by complications. The back cover copy, for instance, argues that *Snake Poems* is "the first time a contemporary writer has returned to the Aztec heritage, empowering himself not only as a translator and commentator but as a medium in the tradition of poet as a shaman."[76] The claim of it being the "first" requires some revisionist history. As Alfred Arteaga writes in *Chicano Poetics,* "it is common for Chicano poetry to mention something Indian."[77] But also Nahuatl is not a dead language and literature has been continuously written and published in it in Mexico and South America. Natalio Hernández is but one example of a contemporary writer in the 1980s and 1990s who wrote in Nahuatl. But while the back cover copy begins by suggesting a possible heritage claim to Aztec culture (and many of the poems suggest something similar), it also alludes to Francisco X. Alarcón's possible relation to Ruiz de Alarcón.

That all three of these works include indigenous language passages appropriated from seventeenth-century works is telling. For anyone interested in languages and linguistic diversity, the seventeenth century, like the end of the twentieth century, is a pivotal moment and it is no coincidence that three crucial works written at the end of the twentieth century rest on top of works written in the earlier century. The 1648 Peace of Westphalia established the idea of the nation-state and the seventeenth century was "the age of exploration," which forecasted the colonialism to come. And the number of languages spoken in the world was at its height at the beginning of the seventeenth century. Further, the European colonization that defined the seventeenth century and that would decimate many cultures and their languages, a process still ongoing at the turn of the twenty-first century, had just begun. There was also in the seventeenth century an intense awareness and fascination with dialects, a love of neologism, and an interest in the languages that Europeans were encountering in the Americas. The English language in the seventeenth century was undergoing significant changes that might best be thought of as setting into motion English's ascent into a global language by the end of the twentieth century. Between 10,000 and 25,000 new words were introduced into English in the 150 years before Williams wrote. For M. M. Bakhtin, the century or so preceding these books was a period characterized by a triumph of heteroglossia over monolingualism, the death of official Latin, a grassroots vernacular rebellion that was directly enabled by scholars and writers and that also enabled the creation of new genres, such as the European novel.[78]

Ruiz de Alarcón's *Treatise on the Heathen Superstitions* and Williams's *A Key into the Language of America* have complicated histories that surely influenced these three contemporary writers to turn to them as sources for their work. Williams's *A Key into the Language of America,* a sort of Narragansett dictionary, is a record of early contact between the Narragansett tribe and the English. He wrote this book in what is now Providence, Rhode Island. Williams is both a hero and an antihero in histories of the time. Along with some 9,000 others, he immigrated to Boston in 1631 in the Great Migration. He was expelled from Massachusetts in 1635 for nonconformism. He bought land from the Narragansett and established Providence Plantation in what is now Rhode Island. He was both an outspoken advocate of Native American rights (as the Rhode Island tourist bureau likes to remind) and yet in 1672 he also sold a number of Native Americans into involuntary servitude (less mentioned by the same tourist bureau).

While *A Key into the Language of America* is a unique work, it is also very much a product of its time. The conventions of the dictionary as we know it today were not yet established in the seventeenth century (Johnson first proposed his *Dictionary* in 1747) and as a result, as Patricia Rubertone notes, *A Key into the Language of America* "defies simple categorization."[79] Most of the works on Native American languages that were written at the time are collections of vocabulary words with no grammar. Williams's discussion of language is more sophisticated. As the title indicates, his book is written before English gets established as *the* language of the Americas. He acknowledges language change, noting moments when English has already entered into Narragansett and he preserves language's multiplicities, noting that "sometimes there are two words for the same thing (for their Language is exceeding copious, and they have five or six words sometimes for one thing)."[80] For its contemporary readers, it served as a how-to manual for contact and trade. And for many years it was considered a key anthropological work, providing an unusually detailed record of Narragansett culture in the mid-seventeenth century.

Just as Stevens and Waldrop chose a work loaded with questions of both language and colonialism as a source for their works, so does Alarcón. The proper name overlap is an obvious point of connection, or as the back cover puts it, "intrigued by the manuscript and by the disquieting possibility that Ruiz de Alarcón might be a distant relation."[81] Like Williams's *A Key into the Language of America,* Ruiz de Alarcón's *Treatise on the Heathen Superstitions* is exemplary of seventeenth-century attitudes, but of Spanish ones, the same that led Elio Antonio de Nebrija in his 1492 Spanish *Gramática* to proclaim language as the instrument of empire. Ruiz de Alarcón came to the attention of the Holy Inquisition in Mexico City for his exceptionally harsh autos-da-fé. There was an investigation and the Inquisition, in one of those painful ironies that are throughout colonial histories, decided that he had not acted out of malice and so promoted him to ecclesiastical judge. One of his duties was to report back to the church on pagan practices. The result was his *Treatise on the Heathen Superstitions.* The treatise was a document to identify pagan behavior, and as a result it includes many examples of Nahuatl rituals in Nahuatl with Spanish translations. The *Treatise on the Heathen Superstitions* is written in six treatises that describe various religious practices, various spells for hunting and fishing, for emotions, and for health. Like Williams's *A Key into the Language of America,* it is often considered to be a valuable anthropological work, despite its obvious biases and distortions, as it is one of few moments where seventeenth-century Nahuatl works are transcribed in their contemporary moment.

Despite these endless examples, this literature in English that includes other languages is not recognized by scholars as a "thing," much less as antistate. Among scholars of twentieth and twenty-first-century literature the language of composition for literary production tends to get overlooked as a neutral or a default. It is so unattended that when Michael Bérubé notices something similar to what I am saying, he suggests that it will likely not be until 2525 that "the distinction between modernism and postmodernism will come to seem much less significant than—or will perhaps be subsumed by—the division of the century into periods before and after the global expansion of English-language literature."[82] So a minor subargument here: The scholarly tendency to segregate literature by racial / ethnic identity has made it difficult (for scholars in particular) to see the development of this literature in English that includes other languages, to notice connections and overlaps, to notice the development of a literature that critiques global English and also refuses the representational concerns of state-sponsored U.S. multiculturalism that was becoming the dominant national tradition at the time. The tendency to group this literature with other multicultural texts does it a disservice in that it imposes a complicit nationalism on the literature, rather than a resistance. In other words, even while Waldrop's and Stevens's books are so similar, the tendency has been to read Waldrop as an experimental writer indebted to European modernism and Stevens as a Native American writer indebted to native traditions, not as two writers among a number who are both attempting to write a critique of English language expansionism within English. Scholars who do notice the overlap between these two works tend to notice it as idiosyncratic.

I started this book with a question about whether a literature that refuses to be Standard English–only could imagine an other-than-national community. At the time I thought the answer could possibly be yes. Now my argument about this literature is somewhat contradictory. It is built around two opposing ideas: that there is a thriving, complicated, aesthetically resonant other-than-national literature written at the turn of the century that is every bit as formally and aesthetically revolutionary as Dante. And yet, this literature has limited reach, is restricted to a narrow audience, as it is read mainly by those in higher education and others who have a professional relationship to literature. It is not just that that this literature is not incubated within and for political movements as literature; it is not seen by resistance movements as meaningful to their goals.

Work by native writers might be a possible and telling exception here. Apio's plays, for instance, were written to encourage discussion about sovereignty. He literalizes this in *Kāmau A'e*: after characters begin an occupation of the land, there is an intermission and actors are directed to "remain in character, talking to the audience as if they are all tourists."[83] And Trask, of all the writers I mention, has been the clearest antistate antagonist. She has been actively involved in Ka Lahui Hawai'i, a grassroots initiative for Hawaiian sovereignty that was founded in 1987. Her street protest presence has been contestatory. She was often seen at protests in the 1990s carrying a sign that said "Haole Go Home." As I previously mentioned, she claims her poetry is "a furious, but nurturing aloha for Hawai'i."[84] And her poetry is angry, resistant. "Racist White Woman" from *Light in the Crevice Never Seen* begins like this:

I could kick
your face, puncture
both eyes.

You deserve this kind
of violence.[85]

While there is a debate to be had about whether literature is as important to the current sovereignty movement as it was to say culturalist movements in the 1960s and 1970s, I would not want to deny the possibility that this literature is a furious aloha. But it is worth noticing that this is yet another example of the importance of literature to nationalism (in this instance to a liberatory nationalism, not to an existing nation-state). And even in this context it is muted. The "Hookupu a Ka Lahui Hawaii," the Ka Lahui Master Plan for Hawaiian sovereignty, mentions the right of Native Hawaiians to freely pursue "economic, social and cultural development."[86] But the role of literature is not specified. And it also is telling that while the plan includes David Malo's "Pule Hō'ōla," the accompanying material pointedly calls it a prayer, separating it from the merely literary.[87]

But outside of isolated examples, despite how critical this literature is of globalization—it has critiqued globalization not just in content but has let critique define its forms—it is more or less irrelevant to the fairly significant, unusually militant antiglobalization movement such as the 1988 annual meetings of the International Monetary Fund (IMF) and the World Bank in Berlin, the G7 in Paris in 1989, the fiftieth anniversary celebration of the IMF and World Bank in Madrid in 1994, the January 1, 1994, declaration of war by the Zapatistas against Mexico, or the dramatic rising up in Seattle against the World Trade Organization in 1999. As David Graeber jokingly points out, it is puppets, not literature, that police fear in this time.[88] The intensity of this disconnect is somewhat new. In the next chapter, I turn to literary history to tell a story of literature's stubborn relationship to the state, a history that defines and shapes understandings of literature today.

CHAPTER TWO

Stubborn Nationalism

Example One, Avant Garde Modernism

⚜

I WAS TAUGHT A sort of proto-Casanovian version of literary history in graduate school. I was taught that there were two traditions that defined U.S. literature: modernist and New Critical. The New Critical one was literary nationalism and the modernist one was resistant. The story went something like this: once upon a time, a time post-Westphalia, literature was mostly national. Then these various national traditions were challenged by the internationalism of modernism. Often this story located the beginnings of this resistance in the publication of Paris-based U.S. American Gertrude Stein's *Tender Buttons* in New York in 1914. But as it argued that modernism was an international challenge to national literatures, it was often also located in 1909 when Italian Filippo Tommaso Marinetti proclaimed the beginnings of futurism in French on the front page of *Le Figaro* or in 1910 when English Roger Fry organized his exhibition *Manet and the Post-Impressionists* in London or . . .

Modernism's writers were not only international, if one can use that word to describe their Euro-American friendships, but the literature they wrote often used syntactically atypical grammars (often ones that mimic the language conventions of those new to a language) or was composed in more than one national language, dialect, or idiolect. The exemplary writers of the U.S. version of this tradition might be Stein, Langston Hughes, T. S. Eliot, Ezra Pound, or Claude McKay, all of whom worked in and also against various genre and formal conventions and all of whom also spent time in Europe. Paris was the obvious center here.

Modernism, in this story, challenged the reigning national traditions of a variety of European and American nations all at once. In the United States, the challenge was to the traditions that would eventually be grouped under the term New Criticism (or more specifically the Agrarians) and the legacy of this tradition is sometimes umbrella-ed by Charles Bernstein under the term "official verse culture."[1] The writers that would come to be associated with New Criticism were the writers who stayed in the United States, who used Standard English, who had few international intentions when it came to literary forms, and who—after a brief flirtation with modernism—rejected its internationalism. They, as Angie Maxwell notes in *The Indicted South,* rejected modernism so as to champion "white southern economic values" and they "established a rhetoric of rural southern superiority and resistance to modernization."[2] They got the U.S. academic jobs and the government grants and prizes. The legacies of this sort of tradition and the control that it continues to wield over U.S. literary institutions is why Bernstein's term is so resonant. The exemplary writers in this tradition are Randall Jarrell, John Crowe Ransom, and Robert Penn Warren. Nashville, not Paris, was the center.

I carried this division in my suitcase with me to my first job at the University of Hawai'i at Mānoa. When I taught twentieth-century literature, I often began with this division. I would draw a horizontal line that I then loaded up with various terms, attempting to pictorially represent one tradition facing off against the other. So, on the modernism side of the line: Euro-American internationalism / Stein, Pound, Hughes, McKay / urban (Paris) / alternative Englishes, languages other than English / disruption / revolutionary and resistant. And then on the New Criticism ṣide: U.S. nationalism / Jarrell, Ransom, Warren / agrarian (Nashville) / Standard English / unity / complicit and national.

This story was, like all overviews, full of exceptions and it was easy to quibble about the terms here and we often did in these classes. Pound combined all the internationalism and aesthetic forms of modernism (writing in more than one language; claiming and reforming a world lineage; etc.) with a reactionary fascism. Hughes, depending on the poem, might belong as much to the New Critics as to the modernists. The McKay of the Harlem Renaissance, of the gorgeous formalism of "If We Must Die," similarly might belong more to the New Critical side while his early works in dialect such as *Songs of Jamaica* and *Constab Ballads* and his later *Banjo,* a "story without a plot," would put him somewhat formally with the modernists. (Or *Banjo* might at least. His first two books, written while he was very young and still in Jamaica, have especially complicated inception stories and reception; Walter Jekyll, the British expatriate who helped McKay to publish the books and wrote the introduction to them saw them not as modernist but as "charmingly naïve love-songs."[3]) But these sorts of quibbles are specific. I was more interested in the broad outlines of this story, what it enabled or avoided when we thought about and with contemporary literatures. It remains a powerful story. It continues to define, although often different terms are used. Sometimes the difference is presented as one between "experimental" and "mainstream." Sometimes it is also called the difference between language and lyric. Or sometimes more idiosyncratic terms are used, such as raw and cooked (which Robert Lowell used in his acceptance speech for the National Book Award in 1960) or School of Quietude and post-language (used by Ron Silliman more recently).[4]

There is much that is right about this story. Perhaps it is as much right as it is wrong and myopic. The rightness of this story is that it is about two dominant traditions of U.S. literature, two often oppositional traditions that continue to this day to compete over the spoils that are academic jobs, grants, prizes, and other sorts of other-than-marketplace remuneration that come to writers of prestige literature. This division, of course, ignores a huge amount of poetries that develop later in the century and the continued use of this divide to define literary study is more troubling when talking about U.S. literatures from the 1960s forward. But it is also somewhat wrong about the turn of the twentieth century in that it implies that modernism is more or less an aesthetic revolution formed in resistant dialogue with dominant national traditions and that modernism's aesthetics are European and original. I instead locate the development of modernism's forms in the large sweeping changes that colonialism brought to Europe. Modernism in its moment of conception is thus somewhat "resistant" (or "autonomous" to use Casanova's terms), although in a very measured way.

It was teaching at the University of Hawai'i at Mānoa that helped me to think about modernism as a literature that, while not anticolonial, was shaped by the aesthetic forms and concerns of the colonies. I was a new teacher so I had to teach a lot of introduction to literature courses. In one course, Poetry and Drama, I assigned *Antigone,* Shakespeare's *The Tempest,* his sonnets, Stein's *Tender Buttons,* and Apio's *Kāmau.* The texts that I chose were somewhat accidental, a combination of meeting the requirements (a Greek and a Shakespeare), works I had taught before (*Tender Buttons*), and one that I wanted to think more about (*Kāmau*). Of all these works, it was mainly Stein that students forced me to read in new and exciting ways. As they kept pointing out, it makes more sense to think of the linguistic pyrotechnics of Stein and avant garde modernism less as an aesthetic project and more as a reaction to nineteenth-century national literary conventions, more as registering the large-scale changes that were the result of colonialism. They did not say it like that but that is what they meant. The way they said it was by writing seminar papers, for instance, that compared *Tender Buttons* to the Kānaka Maoli concept of hakalau, of looking astray. Or by claiming that *Tender Buttons* was written in a form of Pidgin, a European pidgin. Out of this I realized, as Peter Quartermain points out in *Disjunctive Poetics,* that Stein's multilingual childhood and her adult life in voluntary exile had more to do with her writing than I had previously realized.[5] But I also realized that the forms of avant garde modernism that I had been seeing as an ahistorical aestheti-cism (which I often called "new" or "strange") were actually, as my students kept patiently pointing out to me, the same tech-niques used in oral literary traditions. So Stein's linguistic pyrotechnics were not, in other words, just personal or idio-syncratic, they resembled the large-scale changes to thought and aesthetics that happened because of colonialism. And no-ticing this influence told a very different story about avant garde modernism.

There are, as these students in Hawai'i helped me realize, certain literary forms that tend to develop in response to colonialism. Colonial and occupying governments—aware of how tightly languages can carry identities and preserve cultures and thus resistance to colonialism, and also aware of how languages and the cultural products created out of them (the written word and song) play significant roles in the creation of national belonging—commonly impose their language, through a lethal combination of law and education, on the colonized territory. Understanding the ramifications of this defined a number of the more significant works of literary scholarship in the 1990s. Gauri Viswanathan's *Masks of Conquest: Literary Study and British Rule in India,* for instance, is a detailed study of this process in India, of how "English literary study had its beginnings as a strategy of containment."[6] And many postcolonial scholars note the resulting impact of this containment and resistances to it. Bill Ashcroft, Gareth Griffiths, and Helen Tiffin in *The Empire Writes Back* survey these various traditions and notice them as developmental: "Post-colonial literatures developed through several stages which can be seen to correspond to stages both of national or regional consciousness and of the project of asserting difference from the imperial centre."[7] In this they are echoing Frantz Fanon. In "On National Culture" Fanon also theorizes the role of the "native writer" as developmental: first the writer writes under the influence of empire's literatures, next the writer turns away from these traditions and often toward folk traditions, finally then the writer realizes they must write a fighting literature.[8] Whether this developmental frame holds or not, the literatures that are created in colonies, both that written by colonizers and those written by the colonized, tend to be very aware of language politics. Some of these literatures use standard language in order to support colonialism but some use it to speak an anticolonialism that will be legible to imperial centers. And at the same time some write a multilingual literature and some write only in the languages that were present before colonization. These later two options rarely are used as an agent and justification for colonialism. (This sort of assumption, that writing in an other-than-standard language is one of the ways that writers amplify their autonomy from the state, also defines Casanova's observations.)

The attention by scholars to how literature written in colonial situations often is written in opposition to an imposed nationalism makes sense for the postcolonial situations that Ashcroft, Griffiths, and Tiffin were surveying. But what the students in Hawai'i notice about *Tender Buttons*—that avant garde modernism is a literature written in and out of empire but written out of a moment when the cultures of colonialism are filtering into Europe—is something different, something that notices that colonialism not only shaped the literary traditions of colonies, but also of empire.

The students in Hawai'i were not the first to notice this. When Virginia Woolf writes about this time, she does it like this: "On or about December 1910 human character changed."[9] She is at this moment telling a story about the origins of the aesthetic revolution that is modernism. It is often said that she is thinking about Roger Fry's November 1910 exhibition *Manet and the Post-Impressionists,* an exhibition that showcased works by Gaugin, Manet, Matisse, and Van Gogh. But Fry's exhibit goes unmentioned by Woolf and in the essay she locates December 1910 in how "all human relations have shifted—those between masters and servants, husbands and wives, parents and children."[10] Hierarchies were shifting, in other words. And this, she asserts, changes literature. In 1910, she continues "the smashing and the crashing began," a smashing, she metaphorizes, of the house of the Edwardian novel.[11] Her examples are James Joyce and Eliot. She calls Joyce a window breaker. She does not mention how Stein's *Tender Buttons* tore into and through the domestic space, but she might have. Aesthetic revolutions, Woolf realizes, are not just about aesthetics. They are poked and prodded into existence by social forces and influences. On or about December 1910 could easily be about the rapidly growing worker's movement, the on-going strikes and unrest that began in Russia in 1905 and would culminate in a revolution in 1917. Or the beginnings of the Great Migration in the United States. Or the mass protests by women in Britain that led to new social agendas. Or the end of the Edwardian period and its conspicuous consumption.

Not just Woolf notices this smashing and crashing. All sorts of modernists say something about changing human relations and the impact these have on literary form. Stein also attempts to make sense of this when she writes in "What Is English Literature?": "As the time went on to the end of the nineteenth century and Victoria was over and the Boer war it began to be a little different in England. The daily island life was less daily and the owning everything outside was less owning, and, this should be remembered, there were a great many writing but the writing was not so good."[12] The Boer War (the 1899–1902 one) is often seen as the beginning of the decline of the British Empire. Although it is not the decline in colonialism: in 1902 still 90 percent of Africa, 99 percent of the Pacific, and 27 percent of the Americas had been claimed as territories by either the United States or a European nation; decolonization would not really begin to happen until the early 1960s. Stein is saying something here in her roundabout way about how those nineteenth-century national literary traditions were feeling a little less than useful in a changing world, and she, like Woolf, locates it in the "the owning everything outside was less owning," or in the dissolution of hierarchies. But unlike Woolf, she seems to also be talking about colonialism: "owning of everything outside."

Also, Eliot's famous maxim "Return to the sources" is about the influence of the literature from the colonies: "as it is certain that some study of primitive man furthers our understanding of civilized man, so it is certain that primitive art and poetry help our understanding of civilized art and poetry. Primitive art and poetry can even, through the studies and experiments of the artist or poet, revivify the contemporary activities. The maxim, Return to the sources, is a good one."[13] Even in the 1930s, when Eliot's work turns from internationalism and an interest in elsewheres to nationalism, he still notices in his lectures at Harvard poetry's ties to oral traditions from afar: "Poetry begins, I dare say, with a savage beating a drum in a jungle, and it retains that essential of percussion and rhythm."[14] As David Chinitz notes, "Primitive culture interested Eliot, however, not only because of its otherness but because of its ostensible lineal relation to modern culture."[15] And in 1942, when Eliot reminds in "The Social Function of Poetry" that no art is more stubbornly national, he follows that declaration by noticing, "A people may have its language taken away from it, suppressed, and another language compelled upon the schools, but unless you teach that people to *feel* in a new language, you have not eradicated the old one, and it will reappear in poetry, which is the vehicle of feeling."[16]

Woolf, Stein, Eliot, all are saying something that anticolonial writers articulate again and again and with more clarity, directness, and complication. Aimé Césaire at the second *Présence Africaine* Congress of Black Writers and Artists talks about culture as "great storehouses of strength from which the people can draw courage in critical moments to assert themselves and to assault their future."[17] As does Suzanne Césaire in "1943: Surrealism and Us" when she links surrealism not just into the European avant garde but also to her "us," to how "the magical power of the ma-houlis will be recovered, drawn forth from living sources. Colonial stupidity will be purified in the blue welding flame. Our value as metal, our cutting edge of steel, our amazing communions will be rediscovered."[18] Her use of future tense is because she is considering what she calls a tomorrow, that eventually there will be this recognition and "finally those sordid contemporary antinomies of black / white, European / African, civilized / savage will be transcended."[19]

Between 1910 and 1959 much of what Woolf might have noticed as beginning would have manifested. World War I accelerated many changes to culture. The first Pan-African Conference was held in 1900 in London. It would set into motion not only the term "pan-African" but also the development of meaningful alliances among the colonized, alliances that would result in decolonization fifty to sixty years later. Subsequent Pan-African congresses would be held in 1919, 1921, 1923, 1927, and 1944. And, of course, the Bandung Conference would be held in 1955. These gatherings were just one part of the network of forces that would result in decolonization.

But not just this. Paris during these years would be a sort of center of this developing anticolonialism. Michael Goebel in *Anti-Imperial Metropolis* locates the "political careers of future leaders such as Zhou Enlai, Ho Chi Minh, or the founding father of Algerian nationalism, Messali Hadj" in how these men were spokesmen for their communities in interwar Paris.[20] Brent Hayes Edwards notes similarly the connections between anticolonial leaders such as Lamine Senghor, Nguyen Ai Quoc (Ho Chi Minh), Jean Ralaimongo, and Louis Hunkanrin and French socialists such as Paul Vaillant-Couturier.[21] Also, labor shortages during World War I led France to recruit over 600,000 soldiers and over 200,000 (some have this number as high as 300,000) travailleurs exotiques from the colonies.[22] Eventually many of these immigrants from the colonies would be repatriated. Tyler Stovall in "National Identity and Shifting Imperial Frontiers: Whiteness and the Exclusion of Colonial Labor after World War I" argues that the repatriation "inadvertently gave racial distinctions a new, and permanent, place in the metropole itself."[23] But as much as racial distinctions, national distinctions (especially between empire and colony) were also established in a new and permanent way at this moment. Although it is, of course, absurd to prioritize one over the other as they work together in a troubling synergy. What matters about this to understandings of modernism is that the 800,000 people that arrived in France from Asia and Africa had ties to other conceptions of the "literary." And the aesthetic gestures of these traditions became a part of the highly literate work of avant garde modernism. These migrations expanded not only the formal conventions of literature but also broke down the conventions that kept high art and low art, different national traditions, and the oral and the literate separated. But it is not just that these cultural forms arrived only through the travailleurs exotiques. As James Clifford and other scholars have already noticed, a number of key anthropological and ethnographic works on other than European culture were published, and these too shaped avant garde modernism. The result, as Simon Gikandi notices in "Modernism in the World," is that "modernism represents perhaps the most intense and unprecedented site of encounter between the institutions of European cultural production and the cultural practices of colonized peoples. It is rare to find a central text in modern literature, art, or ethnography that does not deploy the other as a significant source, influence, or informing analogy."[24]

Another way to understand this story about the other than national possibility of avant garde modernism is by tracing the publication of Stein's work in a journal such as *Transition*. My argument here is one that echoes studies of the literary magazines, such as *Modernism in the Magazines* by Robert Scholes and Clifford Wulfman, that modernism more or less happened in little magazines because certain advances in printing technologies allowed the creation and distribution of independently funded and produced literary magazines.[25] And, more recently, Eric Bulson begins *little magazine, world form* with the observation that "no little magazines, no modernism; it's as simple as that."[26] *Transition* was edited mainly by the polylingual American Eugene Jolas while he lived in Paris.[27] (The editorial history of *Transition* is complicated. Jolas is the only editor who remained an editor for the entire run; he was joined at various moments by Stuart Gilbert, Matthew Josephson, Elliot Paul, Robert Sage, and James Johnson Sweeney.) The journal tellingly documents the concerns of avant garde modernism from the turn of the century to the pre–World War II period as it came out monthly from 1927 until 1932 (after 1932 it came out less regularly, first from the Hague and then from New York, until 1938). In its eleven-year run, it published work by a wide range of writers and artists from a number of different cultures. Looking now at who got published in *Transition,* the journal feels unusually prescient and maybe even unique. A number of works by soon to be major writers in English, such as Stein and Joyce, show up in its pages. The journal publishes close to one hundred and fifty pages of work by Stein, including *Tender*

Buttons and a number of key works such as "An Elucidation," "Studies in Conversation," and *Four Saints in Three Acts,* and more than three hundred pages by Joyce, all of it early drafts of *Finnegans Wake.*

Jolas uses juxtaposition in *Transition* like a loom. He weaves specific located cultures into one variously composed whole by paying attention to formal complications around language, resolutely suggesting that a revolution of the word (as he liked to call the work he collected) is global, cross-cultural, and anti-imperial. The fifth issue, for instance, points to the influence of the colonies on what will eventually be called primitivist work by putting an unidentified painting by Pablo Picasso next to a sculpture called "Statue de la Mort Violente" identified only as "Aztèque" and another sculpture identified only as "Zapethèque." In later issues these juxtapositions become more extreme and more sophisticated. The twenty-fifth volume collects under the title "Inter-racial Documents" a Bororo myth, two "versos mulatos," a Baluba fetishman's head-dress from the Belgian Congo, a figure in granite rock from Costa Rica, an essay from Louis E. Valcárel titled "There Are Several Americas," and two Aztec sculptures. Jolas juxtaposes plastic art from a wide variety of geographic locations and does the same for literature as he publishes work from many different continents and cultures. Crucially, Jolas's juxtapositions point to disparate connections between the art of empire and the art of the colonies, the two-way street of influence, even as his journal is clearly edited from within empire.

It is not just editorial, juxtapositional proximity here. The editorials and reviews and essays of *Transition* repeatedly rehearse this argument that avant garde modernism's forms are reflective of a world changed by colonialism, a world suddenly very much aware of how different cultures and their arts and their languages are entering and shaping European centers, over and over. Jolas's editorials in *Transition* (often cowritten with the various other editors) tirelessly promote the avant garde as he argues that this writing, which at moments he calls a declaration of linguistic independence, was indebted to the disruption of the center. While Jolas does not use the words "imperialism" or "colonialism" or "globalization," he does relate the avant garde to economic and political changes. In a piece titled "Race and Language," Jolas writes of the poet in the generic: "He builds the creative language of the future by consciously welding together the elements of all the languages in flux due to the interracial synthesis now going on. He seeks a new syntax and vocabulary in order to give voice to the enormously complicated world of psychic changes that are the result of the biological politico-economic metamorphoses today."[28] In another moment he writes, this time with co-editor Elliot Paul, in homage of the ongoing dialogue between the arts and literatures of various nations that so defines the time: "We insist upon the supra-national conception which reveres and protects the indigenous and the individual, which welcomes the vigor of the primitive and appreciates the refinement of high civilization, which can contemplate the occidental dynamism in oriental tranquility, aware of the complementary qualities of beauty and ugliness, of the moment's share in eternity, of unexplored dimensions."[29] His term "supra-national" in particular interests me as it suggests a transcending of national boundaries. It is not just Jolas who speaks so optimistically. Indian writer Raja Rao, in response to Jolas's questions about the crisis in language, again notes the crises in "economic and political spheres" and the resultant revolution in language that is happening in the twenty-third issue. And issue number twenty-five has an essay by Cuban writer and anthropologist Fernando Ortiz on "Jitanjafores in

Cuba" (jitanjafora is a term Mexican writer Alfonso Reyes used to describe what might now be called "sound poetry") that clearly locates the origins of the sound poem, a form much loved by Dadaists, in the past and in Cuban traditions. There is a poignant moment in the second issue of *Transition* where the translator Victor Llona hypothesizes in a lovely and unwieldy sentence that "in the year 1948 or thereabouts, when the time has come to paint a comprehensive panorama of the literary activity in the decade immediately following the war, it will be found, I believe, that its most striking characteristic was a determined straining towards an interpenetration of languages and other racial elements such as had never before been attempted or even dreamed of."[30] He is wrong, of course. In 1948 or thereabouts: Northrup Frye's *Fearful Symmetry: A Study of William Blake,* Cleanth Brooks's *The Well Wrought Urn,* and W. K. Wimsatt's *Verbal Icon: Studies in the Meaning of Poetry* were published.[31] Very little scholarly attention was given to avant garde modernism.

Reading *Transition,* it is not that hard to recognize that those classic avant garde modernist forms—polyvocality, disjunction, repetition, unconventional syntax, lack of a narrative arc—are the same forms that oral literatures use. Even as for years many literary scholars argued for Stein's uniqueness and avoided putting an oral poem from the colonies next to something by Stein, avoided understanding them as having that same direct relationship that there is between Picasso's *Woman's Head* and the Fang mask that so famously influenced it. As North notes, "the other difference between Picasso and Stein, that his masks were visual while hers were verbal, might not have mattered much either."[32] It is not that Stein was writing imitative oral poetries in a time of high literacy (as one could say, without complaint, of today's spoken word poetry), but she was writing something closer to what Kamau Brathwaite calls (speaking not about Stein but about contemporary poetries) "the *notion* of oral literature," something approximate but not directly imitative, something oral and yet literate.[33]

There are two Steins: a narrative one and a more disjunctive one. But the Stein that appears in *Transition* is the equivalent of *Woman's Head*, the disjunctive one with the atypical syntaxes that closely resemble the various forms of oral literatures from the colonies. Much of this work easily fulfills Walter Ong's by now classic description of the formal characteristics of oral works. The work that Jolas chose to publish was, as Ong notes of oral works, "redundant or 'copious.'"[34] And Stein is attentive to making this repetition, as Ong notices about oral forms, "additive rather than subordinative."[35] Stein's "An Instant Answer or a Hundred Prominent Men," for instance, is built around simple, repetitive syntaxes with few embedded clauses and recognizable patterning. She states at the beginning of this piece that her project is to "select a hundred prominent men and look at their photographs hand-writing and career, and then I will earnestly consider the question of synthesis."[36] And then she begins "The first one is used to something." Then, "the second one and in this case integrity has not been worshipped." Next, "the third one" followed by "the fourth one."[37] And the piece goes on and on up to one hundred. It is as any oral genealogy: both tedious and transformative. There is also work that uses what Ong calls "aggregative rather than analytic" modes: in "Made a Mile Away" Stein provides a "description of all the pictures that have attracted some attention."[38] She then uses what Ong calls formulas, or "parallel terms or phrases or clauses, antithetical terms or phrases or clauses, epithets" such as "Tintoretto and asleep," "Harry giving it a name," "Greuze and mention Gauguin," "Pablo Georges Juan

André as a name," and so on.[39] I also like to think when Stein commands in "Studies in Conversation" to "describe it continually and not as a forethought" that she is describing in a different language what Ong means when he talks about "aggregative rather than analytic modes."[40]

Further, concerns with language, with fluency, with an immigrant relation to culture and language are throughout the *Transition* canon of Stein's work. She is a lover of the cross-lingual homonym, the pun, and the homophonic translation and Jolas published work that was full of this. "An Elucidation" is full of sound-based puns: "Halve Rivers and Harbours, / Have rivers and harbours."[41] "Studies in Conversation" is literally about learning languages: "As studies in conversation. / Studies. / Practicing, practice makes perfect. Practicing, perfect, practicing to make it perfect. Practice, perfect, practice. As perfect. Practice. Perfect. Practice. / Introducing practicing introducing practicing, practicing, introducing, practice introducing. Introducing practicing. Practicing introducing."[42] In "If He Thinks: A Novelette of Desertion" Stein writes of "A pronouncing dictionary of words for vegetables. / A pronouncing dictionary of words for butter and oil. / A pronouncing dictionary for words and vowels."[43] The monolingualism of English, her work points out, is false. Or, as she very well might be putting it in "If He Thinks: A Novelette of Desertion," "I feel that there is a vocabulary and I feel that there is a vocabulary of suspension bridges. We know of at least three varieties and we have very definite preferences. We prefer to cross them and recross them and we come across them."[44]

In 1927, Jolas reprinted *Tender Buttons,* which was first published in 1914 by Claire Marie Editions in a print run of probably no more than 1,000 copies. It was out of print and circulation by 1927. The tendency has been to read *Tender Buttons* as without precedent, as unique, as sui generis (as Perloff calls Stein).[45] But when Jolas reprinted *Tender Buttons* he told a story of influence. He did not just put it in the journal on its own. He insisted on putting it in a larger context, in a section titled "America," which included not only work by other American avant gardists such as A. Lincoln Gillespie but also work from a diverse range of genres and cultures, such as tales of the Aztec and Inca periods, several Mexican statues, a Columbian figure, and a Peruvian bowl. It also included a significant number of Marxists, leftists, or fellow travelers, many of them immigrants, such as Stuart Davis, Matthew Josephson, Isidore Schneider, Elliot Paul, and Kay Boyle. Placed in *Transition,* this is an entirely different *Tender Buttons,* one that is the literary equivalent of the smashing and the crashing of the house of the novel that Woolf notices.

There are a whole bunch of obvious things to say about *Tender Buttons.* It is written in what one might call prose, the word that is often used to describe sentences that do not follow realist conventions and instead have poetry's associational drive but not its line breaks. While it uses fairly simple language in that there are few words that require a dictionary, it indulges in a lot of grammatical variations. It runs on: "Callous is something that hardening leaves behind what will be soft if there is a genuine interest in their being present as many girls as men."[46] It hangs fire in fragments: "Roast potatoes for."[47] It frequently indulges in a fragmented listing: "An elegant use of foliage and grace and a little piece of white cloth and oil."[48] At moments it even manages to run on in fragments: "Cold pails, cold with joy no joy."[49] It has a definitional desire. But it is a complicated desire. Things get defined all the time. "Sugar," for instance, is first "A peck a small piece."[50] And then Stein follows with a list of negatives, "not privately overseen, not at all not a slice, not at all crestfallen and open, not at all mounting and chaining and evenly surpassing, all the bidding comes to tea."[51] Sometimes all is grammatically set up for a definition but the words seem to have only the vaguest relation to each other: "Nickel, what is nickel, it is originally rid of a cover"; "Rhubarb is susan not susan not seat in bunch toys not wild and laughable not in little places not in neglect and vegetable not in fold coal age not please"; "A blind agitation is manly and uttermost."[52]

It might be easiest to think of *Tender Buttons* as a sort of novel of manners in reverse: one that shows the space of the novel of manners and not the niceties and aggressions and passions and conversations between humans that are the novel of manners. It is especially telling that there is no hint of a nation-state and only the vaguest hint that it is the turn of the century, even as it is clearly an imperial space, a space located within empire, a bourgeois interior, full of objects such as seltzer bottles, dresses, hats, umbrellas, tables, books, with a kitchen full of the proteins and the luxuries, such as roast beef, chickens, pastry, and cocoa. There is no obvious narrator. And while the domestic space is often seen as a female space, and there are some moments where gender shows up ("Mildred's umbrella"; "A long dress"; "A petticoat"; "A little called Pauline"; etc.), the space does not feel particularly gendered. There is also no sign of domestic labor, no sign of who is doing the cooking, the cleaning. That this space is so fractured, so broken, seems suggestive of something. And it seems safe to say that one way to read *Tender Buttons* is as an attack on the novel of manners. In this realm, it makes a certain sense to think of the linguistic pyrotechnics of *Tender Buttons* not just as a reaction to nineteenth-century national literary conventions, not just as an immigrant's personal linguistic disorientation but also as registering, whether intended or not, the systemic crisis that was colonialism. The opening line of "Rooms" is "Act as if there is no use in a centre."[53] And to act as if there is no use in a center might require noticing that Europe is no longer the center because the cultures of the peripheries have remade and decentered it. To act so that there is no use in a center possibly begs the question of origin and of influence. It could suggest venturing into the world with a shared, even if asymmetrical, concern in the disruptions of the world, one that foreshadows William Butler Yeats's 1919 line that "Things fall apart; the centre cannot hold" and Eliot's 1922 line that "These fragments I have shored against my ruins."[54]

Jolas's decision to place *Tender Buttons* in an exploration of the transnational cultural flows is probably more provocative today than it was in 1927. In her time, Stein's work is easily recognizable as other than national (or in other words, it fits a Casanovian-esque frame), even as there is no agreement on how to read her work. Whether friend or foe, those who discuss her work at the beginning of the twentieth century tend to agree that it is anarchic. Edith Sitwell defends Stein as "bringing back life to our language by what appears, at first, to be an anarchic process."[55] Max Eastman attacks in the libertarian journal *The Freeman,* using her work as a prominent example of what he calls "the non-communicative art," or "mumbo-jumbo," and as he does this he indulges in terms that might today be used by conservative pundits to describe an anti-civ anarchist: Stein is "part of that general surrender of mental and moral integrity to crude primitive and unillumined states of passion which threatens our whole Graeco-Christian civilization with ruin. I think this will seem quite obvious to future historians if history survives."[56] Laura Riding defends, perhaps, the primitive possibility (in an article that again uses the word "anarchism" to describe Stein's work):

"Gertrude Stein, by combining the functions of critic and poet and taking everything around her very literally and many things for granted which others have not been naïve enough to take so, has done what everyone else has been ashamed to do. No one but she has been willing to be as ordinary, as simple, as primitive, as stupid, as barbaric as successful barbarism demands."[57]

When scholars have noticed something about how colonialism was changing European cultural forms (a discussion that has happened more among art historians than literary scholars), they have tended to celebrate it as influence or condemn it as appropriative violation. I am less interested in judging this moment. And while I am much more hesitant than someone like Woolf even about modernism's possible resistance, I do want to hold on to how, if nothing else, modernism was a literature that knew itself as something other than national and was under an other than national influence. But I do want to note that it would be absurd to proclaim that avant garde modernism in its early moments was saying the "right" thing about anything really, which might just point out something obvious: that Euro-American modernism's relationship to the art forms of the colonies is an uneasy one. These encounters seep into early Euro-American modernist works sideways, sometimes showing up in atypical juxtapositions, at other moments appearing in the use of the idiosyncratic idiolects, the dialects, and the creoles that were created by colonialism. All that a writer like Stein did was represent the smashing and the crashing that was happening around her as she was writing. This smashing and crashing was imposed on her and she is not in this moment in any way a critic of colonialism. Her writing is merely its residue.

That Stein's work is somewhat inimical to literary nationalism is somewhat true not only in her time, as Sitwell, Eastman, and

Riding noticed, but also true historically. Her work is not really given much attention as a part of "American" literature as that category was constructed through the seminars and survey classes of higher education until the 1970s. And even then she entered the discussion more as a feminist writer and less as an American. It is not until the turn of the twenty-first century that Stein seemed to become a meaningful part of the American literary canon and scholars started to compare her to Thoreau or Whitman. Or so far, so Casanovian.

Casanova, however, does not spend much time in *World Republic of Letters* on Stein, but she probably should have. For whatever Stein was on or about 1910 (perhaps a "revolutionary" or an "autonomous" writer by Casanova's terms), by World War II much of her work was unabashedly nationalist. A subtitle for the yet to be written study of Stein's nationalism might usefully be "From *The Making of Americans* to *Lectures in America*." But it is not just the word "American" or "America" in her titles. Gilbert A. Harrison collected a number of the pithy nationalist things Stein said in *Gertrude Stein's America*. It includes statements like "there is something in this native land business and you cannot get away from it."[58] The book's jingoism is cringe-inducing.

However, it is not just Stein the writer who had some well-articulated nationalist feelings after the war that might have caused Casanova to rethink her conviction that writers turn from Standard English so as to pursue autonomy. Casanova also oddly ignores the way that national governments manipulate, cultivate, and fund what she calls "autonomous" literature to instrumentalize it as nationalist. Or as Christian Thorne notes in critique of Casanova, "Even abstraction has its political uses, chief among them to mime an independence."[59] And Stein's work, despite its atypical syntax and refusal of Standard English, easily functioned as part of U.S. cultural diplomacy, despite, or perhaps even because of, its linguistic innovations. In 1952 the Congress for Cultural Freedom included a play of hers in the month-long *Masterpieces of the 20th Century* festival that it organized in Paris.

Stein's *Four Saints in Three Acts* was just one small part of the United States' fairly significant cultural diplomacy program. While the CIA networks were especially interested in anticommunist leftists (such as Mary McCarthy) and former communists who were willing to openly denounce communism (such as Wright), the beneficiaries of this largess make up a who's who of early to mid-century U.S. culture, everyone from A. J. Ayer to Julia Child to Czeslaw Milosz. Much of the culture part of the Cold War was overseen by the Congress for Cultural Freedom, which was established in 1950. (The name Congress for Cultural Freedom, similar to how the viceroy mimics the monarch, resembles the "Committee for Cultural Freedom," an antitotalitarian organization started in 1939 by James Dewey and Sidney Hook that was opposed to both the Soviet Union and Nazi Germany.) The Congress for Cultural Freedom was active for over seventeen years. After a 1967 *New York Times* exposé (following up on a story first published in the journal *Ramparts*) that the congress was a front group for the CIA, the CIA turned the congress over to the Ford Foundation and its name was changed to the International Association for Cultural Freedom.[60]

Frances Stonor Saunders documents the events organized by the Congress for Cultural Freedom in exhausting detail in *The Cultural Cold War.* She notes that "at its peak, the Congress for Cultural Freedom had offices in thirty-five countries, employed dozens of personnel, published over twenty prestige magazines, held art exhibits, owned a news and features service, organized high-profile international conferences, and rewarded musicians and arts with prizes and public performances."[61] There are so many parts to this machine that it is almost impossible to summarize or understand them all. I have pieced together the story I am attempting to tell here from a wide variety of sources so as to suggest the extended reach of these forces. While a number of scholars have done crucial archival and historical work on this story, few have attempted to consider not only how these forces overlap and amplify each other but also how they resonant and define the last half of the twentieth century (Saunders's study is exhaustive, for instance, but she ends her study with the New York Times exposé).

The CIA's interest in more abstract and avant garde art forms was not limited to Stein. It also included organized tours set up by the Museum of Modern Art of abstract expressionist art and of free-form jazz.[62] This interest in "autonomous" forms seems to have had a lot to do with the Soviet Union. Culture played a big role in the Russian Revolution. In its early months, especially before the Bolsheviks consolidated their power, the revolution embraced the avant garde. Geoff Eley in *Forging Democracy:*

> In 1917, the revolution had released the imagination—a sense of no holds barred, of being on the edge of possibility. . . . It brought an ecstasy of transgression, in which the people occupied the palaces and art suffused the texture of life, dissolving dichotomies between high culture and low. In the vast popular festivals, like May Day 1918 in Petrograd and the Bolshevik revolution's first anniversary in Moscow or the four great Petrograd festivals of 1920, the masses staged symbolic dramas of history, while the

artists seized the potential of the streets—of carnival and circus, puppetry and cartoons, and other popular media. Carrying art to the masses took many forms in 1918–20: the ubiquitous posters; street theater; factory arts groups, with genres of industrial writing and performance; and the "agit-trains" that used art and film to politicize the peasants. The forms were carnivalesque rather than monumental, the aesthetic one of movement rather than order.[63]

Shortly after the 1917 revolution, Anatoly Lunacharsky established Proletkult, an artistic institution that supported artists in the creation of a revolutionary aesthetic and that demanded autonomy from the Bolshevik government in order to do so. In *Culture of the Future: The Proletkult Movement in Revolutionary Russia,* Lyn Mally points out that in the fall of 1920 "the center claimed between four hundred thousand and five hundred thousand members, eighty thousand of those in elite artistic studios" (although she also notes that these numbers are not definitive).[64] Vladimir Mayakovsky's early works, full of revolution and experimentation, come out of this moment. Proletkult was amazingly successful up until 1920, the year it was absorbed into Narkompros (aka absorbed into the Bolshevik government).

Prior to 1920, there was very little meaningful differentiation between art and propaganda. And the Russian Revolution in its beginnings embraced avant garde modernism as one of the forms that a revolutionary art might take. But after the Bolsheviks won the Civil War, they began to regulate cultural production. Mally again: "As soon they took power, the Bolsheviks began a structural reorganization of national cultural life. Despite the precarious position of the regime, the state offered funds, physical resources, and food rations to a broad array of revolutionary cultural circles. At the same time, it denied support to institutions whose sympathies were suspect, even intervening to close them down."[65] The murder of Nikolay Gumilev, an anticommunist poet, in 1921 is often seen as the beginning of a fairly significant repression of artists who refused socialist realism or Bolshevik politics. By the time the First Soviet Writers' Congress was held in 1934, it was clear that the Soviet Union's interest was limited to the social realism that Lenin called a "party literature" in his 1905 "Party Organization and Party Literature."[66]

This might not have mattered much to the U.S. government except that the Soviet Union had an extensive cultural diplomacy program. Mayakovsky's tours of Europe, the United States, Mexico, and Cuba in the 1920s, where he met with various socialists and communists, were part of this.[67] And it is possible to argue that as the U.S. Communist Party received funds from the Soviet Union, that the organizations they established such as the John Reed Clubs and magazines like *The Masses* and *Partisan Review* (in its early years) that supported and published leftist work written in the United States were also part of this cultural diplomacy. During these years the cultural diplomacy programs in the Soviet Union and the United States developed symbiotically and often resembled and echoed each other. As the Soviet Union federalized support for the arts, the United States established the Works Progress Administration. As the Soviet Union tended to fund and organize not only national events such as the Soviet Writers' Congresses, but also events like 1949's Cultural and Scientific Conference for World Peace that was held in New York and the First International Peace Conference held in Paris, so the Congress for Cultural Freedom organized the International Day of Resistance to Dictatorship and War in Paris the same year.

Both the United States and the Soviet Union used similar rhetoric, although in different directions. The arguments Karl Radek made about modernism at the 1934 Soviet Writers' Congress—that it was petty bourgeois; that it was not proletarian—was defended as freedom by the United States. The U.S. post–World War II propaganda machine not only supported Radek's analysis that "trying to present a picture of revolution by the Joyce method would be like trying to catch a dreadnought with a shrimping net" (supported because they opposed a worker's revolution) but it also indulged a Casanova-style rhetoric in which experimentation was presented as a sign of the autonomy of the U.S. artist and was a U.S. value.[68] As Barnhisel writes, "The American cultural-diplomacy establishment felt that if European artists and intellectuals migrated to 'Picasso's side,' the West would lose the cultural war. Countering the rhetorical use of the term *peace,* then, the West mustered its own trope: *freedom.*"[69]

After the Works Progress Administration was abandoned during World War II, as Michael Denning notes in *The Cultural Front,* "many arts projects participants moved into the war information agencies."[70] He continues, "the State Department's Division of Cultural Relations was formed in June 1938 to handle cultural exchanges with Latin America; it was joined by the CIAA (Coordinator of Inter-American Affairs) under Nelson Rockefeller in August 1940. The Coordinator of Information, founded in July 1941, gave way to the Office of War Information and the Office of Strategic Services in June 1942."[71] In 1948 Congress passed the Smith-Mundt Act, which both specified the terms of public diplomacy and funded it at the federal level. After World War II, the CIA seems to have done most of the cultural diplomacy work until the establishment of the U.S. Information Services / U.S. Information Agency in 1953. When the U.S. Information Services /

U.S. Information Agency was cut in 1999 under the Clinton administration, cultural diplomacy concerns were folded into the State Department in general (where they remain today).

After World War II, the United States used culture in the Cold War not only to argue that the country supported aesthetic freedom for artists, but also to claim that there was no racism in the United States. The State Department's interest in *Four Saints in Three Acts* was not just in its linguistic autonomy, it also interested them that the play first premiered in the United States with an all-black cast, a decision that seems to have been nothing more than a somewhat problematic exoticized novelty. But Saunders in *The Cultural Cold War* quotes a letter by Julius Fleischmann (a businessman who oversaw one of the many private foundations that were functioning as fronts for the CIA) that explains that the State Department thought that the play could counter the Soviet Union's relentless attention to the United States' poor record on race relations in their cultural diplomacy: "there is also a strong feeling that for psychological reason the entire cast of *Four Saints* should be American Negro: to counter the 'supressed race' propaganda and forestall all criticisms to the effect that we had to use foreign negros because we wouldn't let our own 'out.'"[72] And Barnhisel quotes Nicolas Nabokov (Vladimir's first cousin and Secretary General of the Congress for Cultural Freedom): "More important, the psychological effect of an all American-Negro 'Four Saints' well performed at the Paris Exposition would be, of necessity, most rewarding. It would contradict unanswerably Communist propaganda which claims that the American Negro is a suppressed and persecuted race."[73] Stein's play was, of course, but a small part of the U.S. government's attempts to instrumentalize blackness in cultural diplomacy. The State Department–sponsored productions of *Porgy and Bess,* for instance, in numerous European cities for several years. Ellen Noonan covers this tour in great detail in *The Strange Career of Porgy and Bess*. She writes, "The State Department recognized the power of face-to-face contact and firsthand testimony to counteract—or, some cases, to amplify—criticism of American racial inequality, so it organized speaking tours by some African American writers while vigorously obstructing the ability of others (notably Paul Robeson and W. E. B. Du Bois) to have their opinions heard outside of the United States. This belief in African Americans as effective spokespeople, however, only pertained to a handful of carefully selected individuals."[74]

From the beginning, cultural diplomacy was never limited to just the U.S. government. Much of U.S. cultural diplomacy was and remains privatized. The CIA during the Cold War not only established its own foundations, such as the Congress for Cultural Freedom (so as to appear to be independent), it also worked with a number of high-profile preexisting private foundations such as the Ford and the Rockefeller Foundations toward propagating anticommunism however they could. Saunders claims that over 170 foundations were involved.[75] These relationships, as Eric Bennett notes in *Workshops of Empire,* formed "the privatized face of American foreign policy."[76] The relationship between the State Department and private foundations was so intense that Deborah Cohn, in *The Latin American Literary Boom and U. S. Nationalism during the Cold War,* calls it "an open (and sometimes revolving) door": "John Foster Dulles went from being chairman of the Rockefeller Foundation's board of trustees and the Carnegie Endowment of the International Peace to secretary of state in 1953; McGeorge Bundy served as the White House special assistant for national security affairs from 1961 until 1966, when he became president of the Ford Foundation; and former

secretary of defense Robert McNamara was a Ford trustee. . . .
Dean Rusk offers an even more extreme case: he worked at the
Department of State from 1947 until 1952, when he became president of the Rockefeller Foundation, a position that he left in 1961
to return to Washington as secretary of state."[77]

This alliance between the state and private foundations had a
fairly profound and often overlooked impact on mid-century literary production. As Saunders notes, the CIA through the Congress for Cultural Freedom and a number of private foundations,
such as the Ford, the Rockefeller, the Farfield, and the Hoblitzelle,
both established and infiltrated a number of cultural magazines
in the 1950s and 1960s. The list of journals that the CIA either
seems to have in some way been behind the inception of (either
directly established or the journal was created out of the social
milieus that were formed because of CIA-funded reading rooms
or other cultural organizations), significantly supported, or
manipulated in some way is long and international. It includes
Cuadernos (started in 1943, focused on Latin America), *National
Review* (1950; U.S.), *Preuves* (1951; France), *Freedom First* (1952;
India), *Encounter* (1953; UK), *Paris Review* (1953; U.S.), *FORVM*
(1954; Austria), *Quest* (1955; India), *Quadrant* (1956; Australia),
Tempo Presente (1956; Italy), *Africa South* (1956; South Africa),
Black Orpheus (1957; Nigeria), *Examen* (1958; Mexico), *Cadernos
Brasileiros* (1959; Brazil), *Jiyu* (1960; Japan), *China Quarterly* (1960;
China), *Ḥiwār* (1960s; Lebanon), *Transition* (1961; Uganda), *New
Africa* (1962; South Africa), *The Classic* (1963; South Africa),
Censorship (1964; UK), *Africa Forum* (1964; U.S.), *Mundo Nuevo*
(1966; Latin America), *Aportes* (1966, Latin America), and *Soli-
darity* (1966; Philippines).[78] There were also a series of preex-
isting left-leaning journals that the CIA seems to have infiltrated
or funded in some way, such as *The New Leader* (begun in 1924

as a socialist magazine, it received financial support from CIA front groups in the 1950s) and *Partisan Review* (begun in 1934 as an official Community Party USA journal although it quickly disassociated with the Community Party USA but remained left for a number of years; eventually in the 1950s it received financial support from CIA front groups and became progressively more conservative). And a number of liberal cultural journals—such as *Commentary, Daedalus, Journal of the History of Ideas, Hudson Review, Kenyon Review, Poetry,* and *Sewanee Review*—were either given funds or had a significant number of copies purchased by CIA front groups.[79]

Nothing is consistent and easy to figure out in this story. Most of these journals mix culture and politics. Most were edited for specific, often nationally specific, audiences. Melvin Lasky's editing of *Der Monat,* a monthly cultural journal for German audiences that was airlifted into Berlin after the war, is often seen as a sort of ur-example here. It was created first with Marshall Plan funds and then received CIA funds and then Ford Foundation funds and then CIA funds again.[80] And as Joel Whitney notes in *Finks, Der Monat* was conceived as "a means to help achieve America's foreign policy goals by winning sympathy for its statesmen and cultural creators alike, as well as by ridiculing the common lines of criticism against American policies and assumptions."[81]

The state and the foundations were involved in little magazine production in several ways. Editors often claimed that the CIA's involvement was so clandestine that they never knew about it. Stephen Spender (editor of *Encounter*), for instance, claims not to have known until the *New York Times* broke the story.[82] Although many, such as George Watson, assert he had to have known.[83] Sometimes individuals who were a part of this synergy between the state and foundations suggested editors and editorial direction or vetted editors. Whitney, for instance, points to how the Congress for Cultural Freedom not only founded the *Paris Review* as a front for Peter Matthiessen (who was working for the CIA at the time) but it approved various editors of the *Paris Review* (it approved Frederick Seidel, for instance, but not Roger Klein) and provided a job with the Congress for Cultural Freedom to augment the editor's salary.[84] Sometimes they created new journals. The Ford Foundation hired James Laughlin to found and to edit *Perspectives USA*. Laughlin was well aware that his job as editor of *Perspectives USA* was, he claimed, not "to *defeat* the leftist intellectuals in dialectial combat as to *lure* them away from their positions by aesthetic and rational persuasion."[85] Sometimes funds were given directly to editors and / or journals. The *Paris Review* got at least $20,000 from the congress in 1953 (as Whitney notes, "the equivalent of around $180,000 today").[86] And Laughlin seems to have gotten significant funds for *Perspectives USA*, enough to keep Delmore Schwartz on staff as a literary advisor with a monthly retainer of $550 (the equivalent of close to $5000 a month today). Further, as Barnhisel notes, "When Laughlin requested $2.5 million in 1954 to keep Intercultural running for another four years, the board responded with a terminal grant of $500,000, enough to publish *Perspectives USA* through issue 16 and keep Intercultural afloat until October 1956" (about four and a half million dollars today).[87] This viceroy and monarch relationship shows up again too. Matthiessen, when he begins the *Paris Review* as a cover for his CIA affiliation, in the funding prospectus that he submitted mentions Jolas's *Transition* as aesthetic inspiration: "it will be the best literary quarterly since the TRANSITION of the Hemingway-Pound-Gertrude Stein era."[88]

Casanova points out that those who are from countries that have won wars of position in the world republic of letters tend to think "the world of letters is one of peaceful internationalism, a world of free and equal access in which literary recognition is available to all writers, an enchanted world that exists outside time and space and so escapes the mundane conflicts of human history."[89] The congress relied on this naïve presumption when it created its journals. They were designed to look like the liberal (and anticommunist) journals of the time, so as to amplify liberal (and anticommunist) concerns in a war of position with more left-leaning journals (some with ties to the CPUSA and thus the Soviet Union; some more independent). When Matthiessen claimed he wanted the *Paris Review* to resemble Jolas's *Transition,* the only way to understand this comment is that he wanted to mimic its perceived autonomy, not its support for autonomous literature.

But it is not just that these journals had different editorial concerns. Wars of position are, after all, business as usual in the world republic of letters. But it is important to recognize the impact of the United States' manipulation of the playing field on which the war of position occurred. Certain writers, a fairly significant number, whose work was felt to be aligned with national security concerns were given easy and regular publication venues and were paid for their work in a manner that would let them do more of it. They also received translation support and international reach. This reach shaped both the terrain of "American literature" and literatures of other nations. *Perspectives USA,* for instance, had an astonishing print run of over 50,000 copies for some issues.[90] It was priced below market to encourage purchase. And each issue appeared in English as well as French, German, and Italian.[91] Editors at the time also used amplification provided by these networks to bait authors. Whitney covers in some detail how these journals not only paid writers significant fees for their work but also openly offered the possibility of getting paid by other journals in the extended network of Congress for Cultural Freedom journals for reprint rights. Wright's piece, for instance, on the Bandung Conference that he wrote for the Congress for Cultural Freedom appeared in the space of two months in four different languages in four different magazines (*Preuves, Encounter, Cuadernos,* and *Der Monat*).[92] At another moment Whitney notes how the American Committee for Cultural Freedom was "offering literary agency services at large, telling members that if you write pieces that fit our broader aims of fending off critiques of the United States, and if you are a member or friend of the American Committee, we can help you get published in multiple markets."[93] And certain other writers—those more obvious about their affiliations with leftism or anticolonial resistance—did not receive this support. While I remain unconvinced that these journals were successful as cultural diplomacy, the networks that they created were successful in shaping who is seen as a crucial part of American literary traditions. To this day, writers amplified by these networks are disproportionally represented in the canon of American literature.

James Baldwin's career is a telling example. Standard bibliographies of Baldwin (such as the one in James Campbell's *Talking at the Gates*) have him publishing around forty-five or so articles from 1947 to 1956.[94] Over half of these articles were published in CIA friendly journals such as *Commentary,* the *New Leader, Partisan Review,* and *Encounter.* "Everybody's Protest Novel"— an attack on politically committed literature and an argument that great literature should be free of political content and also the essay that "marked his entrance into the literary world" according to Douglas Field—appeared first in *Zero* (edited by George Solomos under the pen name Themistocles Hoetis).[95] But it was quickly picked up and reprinted by CIA networks: *Partisan Review* published it in 1949 and *Perspectives USA* published it in their second issue in 1953. Sol Stein, Baldwin's childhood friend, edited Baldwin's *Notes of a Native Son* while he was Executive Director of the American Committee for Cultural Freedom (the U.S. local office of the congress).

The standard story about Baldwin is that the civil rights movement radicalized him. But as late as the 1963 Baldwin is still very publicly part of U.S. cultural diplomacy as he appeared on a United States Information Agency–organized panel at the March on Washington (the USIA produced a number of films about the march in an attempt to spin it as yet another sign of American freedoms rather than evidence that the Soviet Union was right to notice that the United States was racist).[96] This, of course, does not mean that Baldwin was a puppet of the state. Baldwin for sure had agency in what he wrote and said when working with the government. And, as is true of the writing he did for more independent journals, much of what he wrote was provocative. But still, the Baldwin that we know, we know because his work was amplified by these networks. There is no discounting that he eventually used the megaphone that these networks gave him against the U.S. government. (His career is interesting in comparison with Wright's who did the opposite.) But the fact that Baldwin became a very public radicalized thinker who was trolling the FBI by claiming he was writing a book that would expose them (at his death there was no evidence that he had ever started this book) should not be read as a reason to dismiss how these networks amplified his work. Rather the opposite. It might be that at the end of the twentieth century one could not become a successfully resistant writer without having at some moment been supported or amplified by the publication and distribution technologies of these networks.

These same networks did not just support some writers but not others. They also meddled in the literature of other nations, especially less stable nations, such as those emerging from colonialism and nations that had strong and possibly revolutionary movements in formation. While it may feel diversionary to turn to African literature in this study of twenty-first-century U.S. literature, the literatures that came out of African decolonization movements had a fairly significant impact on U.S. movement literatures of the 1960s and 1970s. Or as Nicholas Brown puts it, "every discussion that isolates a 'modernist tradition' or an 'African tradition' (the very incommensurability of these terms should warn us of their insufficiency) carries with it an inherent falseness."[97] So in order to understand the potential autonomy of both international modernism and U.S. movement literatures, one has to also understand that the idea that there should be in Africa a form of English-language literary production is something that the CIA not only facilitated but also somewhat controlled on multiple fronts. Before the Congress for Cultural Freedom arrived, the various cultures of Africa had, of course, as robust a relationship to culture as any other peoples. There were, of course, age-old literary traditions. But the nations formed by decolonization movements did not have (and by some measurements would not have for some time) robust publication and distribution networks. Almost all forms of colonialism discouraged or prevented the development of independent publication and distribution technologies. (As late as 1978, Keith Smith notes that the Anglophone publishing industry in Africa was limited to "six or seven British-based multinational companies."[98])

In 1955 the Bandung Conference was held in Indonesia. As far as anyone knows, the CIA was not concerned with African literary production until after the Bandung Conference. Employees of the CIA, of course, were at Bandung; and, as I previously mentioned, Wright was one of them. He was, as Brian Russell Roberts and Keith Foulcher puts it, "*officially* . . . not covering' the conference *for* the CCF but would in a putatively unaffiliated way write several articles on the conference to be published in the CCF's internationally distributed English-, French-, Spanish-, and German-language magazines."[99] (These articles were later published as part of his book *The Color Curtain*.[100]) Also while he was in Indonesia, he facilitated, with the congress's direction, ties between Indonesian writers such as Mochtar Lubis and the congress.

The possible impact the Bandung Conference had on cultural production has not received much attention from literary scholars, despite Diop calling the 1956 *Présence Africaine* congress a second Bandung. This is probably because there is no record of the Bandung Conference that suggests that the discussions that took place were much concerned with the role that culture was playing in emerging decolonization movements and would continue to play as new nations were formed after decolonization. But no matter, the political alliances that would be formed at Bandung would define geopolitics in the mid-century and many of the movements that emerged from the conference would be unusually attentive to the role that culture might play in decolonization and its accompanying liberatory nationalist movements. While most of the scholarship on cultural diplomacy during the Cold War has focused on understanding the CIA's involvement in cultural politics as part of U.S. anticommunism during the Cold War, it is also important to recognize how much of the Cold War was also a fight for the hearts and heads of the newly emerging nations that were formed out of decolonization struggles of the mid-century.

But whatever the motivating event, whether one sees it as Bandung or as *Présence Africaine*'s second Bandung or both, the Congress for Cultural Freedom attempted either to establish a form of control over emerging English-language publications or created the conditions that allowed an English-language literature to emerge in the late 1950s. And as in Europe, the congress funded the production of journals such as *Black Orpheus* and *Transition*. *Black Orpheus* was begun in 1957 by German immigrant Ulli Beier with a grant from the Ministry of Education in Nigeria's Western Region.[101] Beier received Congress for Cultural Freedom funds to establish *Black Orpheus* and the Mbari Artists and Writers Club in 1961. (Beier had a suggestively outsized role in the creation of English-language literature in decolonizing nations. In 1966, Beier left Africa and showed up in Papua New Guinea to work at the university there. In Papua New Guinea, very similar to what he did in Nigeria, he edited the journals *Kovave* and *Gigibori,* established a small imprint house, and was involved in several cultural centers. His memoir of this is time, *Decolonising the Mind: The Impact of the University on Culture and Identity in Papua New Guinea, 1971–1974,* is another viceroy; it steals its title from Ngūgī's classic essay collection.[102])

It is often mentioned that Beier founded *Black Orpheus* after attending *Présence Africaine*'s 1956 congress.[103] But if this is true, there is literally no way he could have left the congress with the thought that the right thing for a German immigrant to Africa to do was to edit a journal of African writing in English. How to best pursue cultural autonomy was more or less the entire point of the 1956 congress. Aimé Césaire in "Culture and Colonisation" spoke movingly of how colonial governments impose colonial languages so as to further colonialism and destroy local cultures: "The native language, the language learnt at school, the language of ideas, once it ceases to be the official and administrative language suffers a loss of status that hinders its development and sometimes threatens its very existence. . . . When the English destroy the state organisation of the Ashantis in the Gold Coast, they deal a blow to Ashanti culture. When the French refuse to recognise as official languages Arabic in Algeria or Malgache in Madagascar, thus preventing them from achieving their full potentiality in the modern world, they deal a blow to Arab culture and Madagascan culture."[104] And he was not the only delegate there who spoke of cultural autonomy as a meaningful part of anticolonialism. Léopold Senghor also spoke about the importance of maintaining local languages and asserted that "language is a power in Negro Africa" in his talk "The Spirit of Civilisation."[105]

But whatever motivated Beier—whether he was motivated by the CIA or by a misguided altruism or by some impossible-to-understand motive—*Black Orpheus* had a formidable impact on English-language literature in Africa. Looking at who got published in its pages quantifies Andrew Rubin's claims in *Archives of Authority* that writers who worked within these networks saw great benefit to their reputations and recognition. The journal published a number of writers such as Wole Soyinka and Dennis Brutus who would eventually become well known in English-language literatures and who continued to have unusually close ties to the U.S. government. Soyinka, as diplomatic cables report, met frequently with U.S. intelligence, and a diplomatic cable from 1977 writes of Brutus, "THE EVIDENCE POINTS TO HIS BEING A CIA MAN."[106] (Although obviously, this does not mean Brutus was a CIA man, but it does speak to whether he was or was not, and someone in the State Department recognized him as aligned in some way.) Beier also played fast and loose with the category of Nigerian literature. Beier's commitment to the creation of an English-language Nigerian literature was so peculiarly intense that he also wrote some of the work in the early issues under a series of pseudonyms (no one is sure how much but Peter Benson in *Black Orpheus, Transition, and Modern Cultural Awakening in Africa* says Beier was through his pseudonyms the "dominant voice" for the early years of the magazine).[107] In one of the more absurd moments, Beier wrote a review of his wife Susanne Wenger's art in blackface under the name of Sangodare Akanji and compared her work to Senghor's as he argued that Wegner's was authentically African.[108]

Transition's history is somewhat similar. Rajat Neogy was born in Uganda to parents who had immigrated from India. He began *Transition,* supposedly influenced by *Black Orpheus,* in 1961 and he began receiving Congress for Cultural Freedom funds in 1962.[109] In *The Rise and Fall of* Transition *Magazine* Emmanuel Onuora Nwuneli, in one of few attempts to quantify whether CIA funding changed the editorial focus of these journals (some sort of detailed analysis that compares these state journals to the more independent ones is much needed), notices that after *Transition* received CIA funding there was a sharp increase in political articles.[110] In 1967, *Transition* 32 printed a critique of constitutional proposals that the Ugandan government was attempting to ratify. This article provoked a debate that continued over several issues. The *New York Times* story about the Congress being a CIA front was also published in 1967. In October 1968, Neogy and several of the authors of the controversial pieces in *Transition* were arrested. The case is complicated (and made more complicated by Neogy's dual citizenship, which the Ugandan government refused to recognize). The Ugandan government claimed that the arrests were not for sedition, but because Neogy (who they considered a foreign national) was publishing a magazine financed by a foreign body that was attempting to sway constitutional proposals. And whether one believes the Ugandan government or not (and there are many good reasons not to do so), that these arrests continue to be portrayed as a sign of *Transition*'s autonomy is somewhat ironic, even if it is true, as Neogy claimed, that he did not know about the CIA funding until after the *New York Times* story. (Tony Hall did an interview with him where he claimed "shock" and "a massive two-month long-depression" after finding out, but some have questioned his claims of naiveté.[111]) Whatever Neogy did or did not know prior to the *New York Times* story, it seems telling that after Neogy was released from jail that he did not renounce his association with the congress. Instead he restarted *Transition* in Ghana with a $40,000 annual budget provided by the newly (re)named International Association for Cultural Freedom (now overseen by the Ford Foundation).[112]

The combination of cultural center and journal was a classic CIA pattern at the time. And it is another example of how these CIA-aligned networks were powerful because they used a diversity of approaches that were full of system redundancy that amplified their concerns. As with the European and American journals, these journals often worked to support the conferences that the Congress for Cultural Freedom organized (and the reverse too). Elizabeth Holt points out quid pro quo translation networks and that some work appeared in *Ḥiwār* and in *Cuadernos* and *Preuves* simultaneously: "a global simultaneity of literary experience as an instantiation of the institution of cultural freedom was held out to prospective CCF authors as an incentive."[113] Similarly, there was no way that *Transition* could not be in dialogue with, and thus shaped by, the "independent" publication programs that the CIA was creating at the time. Nwuneli notes that *Transition* published writing by a number of "members of the Mbari writers club in Ibadan, Nigeria" and that this "boosted the image of *Transition* both nationally and internationally."[114] It is not a crime to have close ties with another government; there are many ways to read this as open-minded and progressive. But that the Congress for Cultural Freedom funded *Transition* is telling not necessarily about Neogy but about how successful the congress (and thus the United States) was at controlling the discourse. Even if Neogy had denied the funds because he found them tainted, it would not necessarily mean that *Transition* could be independent of these concerns.

Much of this work seems to have been facilitated by the South African writer Es'kia (then Ezekiel) Mphahlele who was working for the Congress for Cultural Freedom. It is Mphahlele who established the Chemchemi Cultural Centre in Nairobi and he would be an editor of *Black Orpheus* with Soyinka starting with the sixth (1960) issue. Peter Kalliney in "Modernism, African Literature, and the Cold War" claims that after consulting archival sources "it seems highly unlikely" that Mphahlele knew at the time that he was working for the CIA.[115] I am not that interested in whether the individuals who were caught in these systems were "guilty" or not, but I would add that Mphahlele was someone who had close ties with the State Department throughout his life.[116] Hugh Wilford also points to reasons to be suspicious of the archives. The officers of the American Society of African Culture, for instance, were "conscious about observing front group security protocols."[117]

The Congress for Cultural Freedom in Africa mainly supported African writers who were willing to write in English. The organization held its first conference of African writers in English at Makerere University in Uganda in 1962. Neogy and Mphahlele met at this conference. Many scholars have argued that this conference created African literature in English, which is one reason to take it as seriously as the *Présence Africaine* congresses. Gikandi, for instance, opens his excellent summary of "East African Literature in English" with the 1962 Makerere conference and then attributes *Transition* and the Chemchemi Cultural Centre, which was established by Mphahlele while working for the Congress for Cultural Freedom, as playing a crucial role in the development of this literature.[118] Kalliney claims that the Makerere conference announced "the birth of postcolonial African literature in English" and at the same time "started the debate about the appropriateness of using imperial languages in literary production."[119] There is no reason to discount these histories, but the larger issue of what exactly was birthed is difficult to answer.

Obiajunwa Wali in "The Dead End of African Literature?" (published, of course, in Neogy's *Transition*) argues that the Makerere conference's purpose was to suggest that "African literature as now defined and understood, leads nowhere," how it was presented by the participants to be "merely a minor appendage in the main stream of European literature."[120] Ngũgĩ wa Thiong'o (as J. T. Ngugi) also wrote a piece on the conference that was reprinted in Neogy's *Transition*. His piece is more reportage, not argument, and yet the beginnings of the critique that will eventually provoke him to abandon writing in English for Kikuyu in the 1970s show up when he notes that "the whole conference was almost quiet on such things as colonialism, imperialism, and other isms. In this it differed from the 1956 and 1959 World Congresses of Negro writers, where political discussions clouded the atmosphere."[121] When Ngũgĩ returns to the Makerere conference twenty or so years later in *Decolonizing the Mind* his critique is more pointed: "the crisis of identity was assumed in that very pre-occupation with definition at the Makerere conference. . . . The literature it produced in European languages was given the iden-tity of African literature as if there had never been literature in African languages. Yet by avoiding a real confrontation with the language issue, it was clearly wearing false robes of identity: it was a pretender to the throne of the mainstream of African literature."[122]

The proceedings of the Makerere conference show that Ngũgĩ and Wali are correct, that the Makerere conference was a very dif-ferent conference than the 1956 and 1959 Congresses of Black Writers and Artists. The conference talks barely mentioned lit-erature's possible role in resisting colonialism and instead focused on realism and writing for a "universal audience."[123] J. P. Clark mentions in a report back from the "Working Party on Poetry" that the Mbari Club was instrumental, and as concerns poetry in Africa, that the United States could provide a meaningful model for how to make poetry popular (he does not specify the details of this possible model).[124] And Mphahlele, in an article included in the proceedings that was originally published in *Africa Report* (another congress-funded magazine), presents the conference as in opposition to the more resistant concerns of an-ticolonial writing and as one that supports writing that "does not depend on sterile concepts such as 'negritude' or the 'African personality.'"[125]

Some argue that all that happened in this moment was that the CIA created some cultural centers and conferences and some writers and editors showed up at them and edited some inter-esting journals and wrote some interesting books. Gikandi, for instance, does not bother to mention the Congress for Cultural Freedom in his history of East African literature, even as he attributes the networks that the organization created as foundational. Jeanne N. Dingome in an article on the Mbari Club in Nigeria, begins with the acknowledgment of "the centrality of cultural-autonomy in nation-building."[126] But she then claims that it was the Mbari Club that provided this autonomy, despite the club's "dependence upon foreign initiative and capital" from the Congress for Cultural Freedom, which she calls a "left-wing, non-communist organization."[127] Kalliney and Bulson both minimize the impact. Kalliney, for instance, oddly argues that because of "the secrecy of the funding" and that the patronage was "indirect" the result was "more rather than less autonomy, both politically and aesthetically" for African writers.[128] He even goes so far as to argue that the Congress for Cultural Freedom "consistently supported absolute independence of speech and thought, championing aesthetic autonomy as the embodiment of expressive freedom."[129]

While Kalliney's reasoning is one of the more extreme in that he argues that secretive support from a foreign intelligence agency actually protected the autonomy of these writers to develop an apolitical literature in the modernist tradition, study after study minimizes the impact of this involvement. This is true not just about studies of African literature. Cohn, in her study of the Latin American literary boom, presents a detailed history of how this literature became internationally recognized. In her study the CIA, again working with private U.S. foundations, is there almost every step of the way: it publishes boom literature in its journal *Mundo Nuevo;* it facilitates and funds translations; it works with PEN to host a conference; and it facilitates the entry of boom literature into higher education by providing "more than

$11 million in grants to support Latin American studies between 1962 and 1966 alone."[130] And yet she stresses that "a study focused only on PEN's and the State Department's courting of Latin American writers as opinion molders would deny these writers the agency—and the agenda—that was clearly in evidence in their efforts to establish Latin American literature as a phenomenon worth international attention. The congress brought together individuals from different nations and regions in symbiotic relationships even as it laid bare both the contradictory forces at play in U.S. Cold War cultural politics and schisms in the Latin American left."[131] Even Wilford notes that "the CIA could not always predict or control the actions of the musicians, writers, and artists it secretly patronized."[132]

There is much to appreciate in Cohn's, and other scholars', attention to this agency. The writers and editors who wrote for the congress or presented at their conferences or edited their journals of course would have kept their agency as they did this. There is a good chance that when John Thompson, the Farfield Foundation's executive director and the man who recommended that the congress hire Mphahlele, claims that the editors of these journals were just handed money "with absolutely no strings attached" that he is saying something more truthful than not.[133] There is some evidence that the congress was suppressing content, but it seems to have been more the exception than the rule. Saunders notes some interference when she quotes Christopher Montague Woodhouse (an M16 agent who was part of the team that facilitated the journal *Encounter*) claiming that he was "well aware that the Congress for Cultural Freedom was axing pieces. But I never knew of any formal guidelines for this which were precisely laid down anywhere."[134] Kalliney points to a contract Beier signed with Longman, the UK publisher, that stipulates that the "non-political character of the work will be retained."[135] And Whitney's study points to several additional examples such as John Berger's first novel, *A Painter of Our Time,* being suppressed shortly after publication by Secker and Warburg (the same publishing house that published *Encounter*) and also a piece on China by Emily Hahn that was suppressed from *Encounter.* Cohn reports that the Ford Foundation before funding a PEN conference of Latin American writers asked for "reassurance that participants would not engage in political debates that might compromise the organization."[136] Mary Helen Washington in *The Other Blacklist* points to how Lorraine Hansberry's talk at the 1959 First Conference of Negro Writers (organized by the American Society of African Culture, another CIA-supported organization and the U.S. branch of the *Présence Africaine*–affiliated cultural centers) was suppressed from the society's publication, *The American Negro Writer and His Roots.*[137] But even if none of these examples existed, most of the editors and writers who received support were handpicked by the congress because their views were sympathetic to its concerns. So there should have been little need to censor or regulate.

By dwelling so intently on ephemera—how those who received the funds might have had contestatory personal relationships to the U.S. government (that were often expressed in their writing) or how those who worked for the Congress for Cultural Freedom might have conflicting opinions about what sorts of literature best combat communism or how the American Committee for Cultural Freedom and the Congress for Cultural Freedom did not agree about how much dogmatism one can get away with and still have something not look like propaganda—much of this scholarship overestimates the impact of these ephemeral and internal contradictions and underestimates how these forces build and multiply. Brouillette's work on foreign book donation programs, probably because it is more concerned with history and less with aesthetics, is very much aware of the impact of these manipulations. She notices how in postcolonial nations "local productive capacity was stymied by foreign book donation schemes—which were especially rampant due to allocated Cold War funding for propaganda—as well as by the basic media dominance of the advanced economies."[138] In "UNESCO and the Book in the Developing World," Brouillette mentions the significant role played by UNESCO and others, including

> state-based agencies like the British Council; trade organizations like the International Publishers Association; aid agencies like the United States Agency for International Development (USAID) and the Soviet State Committee for Foreign Economic Relations, both of which had major—aversively interdependent—book donation schemes in place at this time; agents of international political economy such as the World Bank, which was in the 1960s and 1970s advancing visions of development that shaped the kind of aid that the book industries in the developing world would receive; and local book trade representatives who appeared before UNESCO because they sought, for instance, exemptions from international copyright agreements that would have allowed them to publish foreign works in less expensive editions, pointing out that the United States had done the same for the many years in which it studiously avoided adherence to the Berne Convention on International Copyright and thereby built its publishing infrastructure via piracy.[139]

To argue that because the individuals involved were not directly controlled confuses the autonomy of the individual with cultural autonomy. The CIA was not funding so many magazines in other nations by the early 1960s because they had a commitment to good writing or because they valued literary autonomy. These magazines, Rubin notes, were "a way to regulate, sanitize, and co-opt the literature of decolonization"; they took advantage of an emerging "transnational imaginary."[140] Basically, the U.S. government was worried that when Aimé Césaire wrote that "the Martiniquan revolution will be made in the name of bread, of course; but also in the name of fresh air and poetry (which comes to the same thing)" he was right, that poetry could lead to revolution.[141] Or if not Césaire, that Amílcar Cabral was right when he wrote in "National Liberation and Culture" that "the study of the history of national liberation struggles shows that generally these struggles are preceded by an increase in expression of culture, consolidated progressively into a successful or unsuccessful attempt to affirm the cultural personality of the dominated people, as a means of negating the oppressor culture."[142] Or that Fanon was right when he wrote about Keïta Fodéba's "African Dawn" in "On National Culture" and very clearly explained that the poetry valuable to revolution defines "accurately the historic moments of the struggle," when it marks "off the field in which were to be unfolded the actions and ideas around which the popular will would crystalize."[143]

And government publications in which cultural diplomacy is defended say as much over and over. These publications make clear that cultural diplomacy is a crucial part, in that it can be the gentle face, of any sort of imperialism. I will not restate these arguments in much detail, but every time that the Smith-Mundt Act comes up before the U.S. Congress, a rhetoric of cultural exchange as leading to dialogue is used. Or as a report from the Advisory Commission on Cultural Diplomacy states, cultural diplomacy counters the way that "America is viewed in much of the world less as a beacon of hope than as a dangerous force to be countered."[144] But cultural diplomacy reaches both "influential members of foreign societies" and reaches out also to "young people, to non-elites, to broad audiences with a much reduced language barrier."[145]

I am not convinced that cultural diplomacy works, to be honest. But while there is little convincing evidence that the claims made by the Advising Committee on Cultural Diplomacy are true, the fact that cultural diplomacy might not work all that well to win over influential or young members of society is not a reason to discount the vastness of these manipulations and the significant impact that they had on autonomous literary production. If one is an absolutist on the issue of autonomy, it is obvious that these manipulations curbed autonomy. If one believes that literature has a role to play in anticolonial resistance or liberatory nationalism, the same. And if one is Casanovian and sees literature as a series of wars of position, same. Even Thompson understands this. He points out that what the Farfield desired was "an independent publication program."[146] But in hindsight he admits "it was probably in the long run, indirectly and obscurely, part of American imperialism."[147]

Basically, the United States, through the CIA and private foundations, manipulated the world republic of letters to be more amenable to their political concerns. They belittled, as Wali points out, more resistant and autonomous literatures such as Negritude. They amplified a small number of writers whose concerns they felt overlapped their own. And although there is no indication that it was intentional, when it was realized that much of the literature in English in East Africa was in some way funded by the CIA, they also tainted the perceived agency of a number of writers. Everything seems to indicate that they were very successful. Edward Said in *Humanism and Democratic Criticism,* while calling nationalism a "mixed blessing" for humanism (he was, of course, attentive to the role that nationalist literature has played in Palestine), notes how dramatically "Cold War concerns" have shaped the field of literary study: "This is not to say that everyone who worked in these fields was in the pay of the CIA, but it is to say that an underlying consensus about knowledge began to emerge that was scarcely visible then but has, retrospectively, become increasingly evident."[148]

It is somewhat illustrative to compare the U.S. government's relationship to African literature and France's. There was at the time a fairly significant number of magazines edited by colonized citizens who because they were residing or had resided in France had access to its extended production infrastructure. The particular relationship that France had to colonialism—that it was a colonial power; that it did not easily withdraw from its colonies but instead fought two fairly intense wars; that it had such a dramatic in-migration from the colonies at the beginnings of the century— is part of the petri dish that would create these journals. These publications were robust, frequently edited, funded, and distributed independently, and were often communist or anticolonial. Nguyen Ai Quoc, later known as Ho Chi Minh, would begin editing *Le Paria* in 1922. Tiemoko Garan Kouyaté began editing *La Race Nègre* in 1927 and then *Le Cri des Nègres* in 1931. In 1928, Maurice Santineau began *La Dépêche Africaine.* In 1931, the Nardal sisters started *La Revue du Monde Noir.* In 1932, a single issue of *Légitime Defense,* was published by a group of Martinican students in France that included René Ménil, Jules Monnerot, and Étienne Léro. In 1935, Aimé Césaire, Léon-Gontran Damas, and Léopold Sédar Senghor published the also short-lived *L'Étudiant Noir*. In 1941 Aimé Césaire with Suzanne Césaire founded *Tropiques* (this one started in Vichy occupied Martinique). And, of course, in 1947, Diop began the journal *Présence Africaine*. This is a partial list. There are other journals here too.

It is not that the French government did not meddle. Some of these journals, as is understood now, had a more complicated relationship to the French state than others. Phyllis Taoua, who spent some time in the archives of the French Colonial Ministry, notes that the French government was (like the U.S. government) nervous about "any perceived alliance between anti-colonial activists and Communism."[149] As a result, the French Ministry of the Colonies, Taoua notices, sponsored *La Revue du Monde Noir* "as long as they maintained a conciliatory position."[150] *Présence Africaine* had a close relationship to the state from the beginning as Diop was elected to the French senate in 1946, the year before he started *Présence Africaine*. And there were also journals that did not take such a conciliatory position, ones that pursued their autonomy so rigorously that they were censored. The "Declaration" that begins the single issue of the journal *Légitime Defense* states "We consider ourselves totally committed. . . . We rise up against all those who don't feel suffocated by this capitalist, Christian, bourgeois world, to which our protesting bodies reluctantly belong."[151] And *Légitime Defense* was thus quickly censored and the editors were expelled from university and repatriated. *Tropiques* was edited for a time in Vichy occupied Martinique and was briefly banned in 1943.

Still, even the conciliatory French journals that see culture as part of decolonization movements are different in telling ways from journals like *Black Orpheus* and *Transition*. Most obviously, the editors of resistant journals tend to be colonized subjects, not colonizers, who are very much aware of the complicated cultural politics they are negotiating. They also, unlike Beier, do not write a significant number of their articles in blackface. They also tended to be directly concerned with resistance to colonialism (in a way that Neogy's *Transition* was not).

I have wandered somewhat geographically far afield in this attempt to tell a story about contemporary literature. There are many reasons to despair that postcolonial African literature in English is something that has the CIA in it from the beginning (and yet, obviously, this should not be used to necessarily tarnish all the literature in English that gets written in Africa), but this is not a study of African literature so I will leave the ramifications of this up to those who are more knowledgeable. My concerns are with how this shapes contemporary literature in English. Any understanding of what contemporary literature in English might be, requires a multipronged examination of the extended reach of the U.S. state and the social networks and publishing infrastructures. Obviously, U.S. literature, and this is true of any national literature, is not produced in a bubble. U.S. literature is under the influence and in dialogue with African literature in English (and also African literature not in English). And not just African literature . . . Casanova's observation that literature is created out of "incessant struggle and competition over the very nature of literature itself—an endless success of literary manifestos, movements, assaults, and revolutions" is useful here.[152] All literatures, in her telling, are relational, are never "a pure emanation of national identity; they are constructed through literary rivalries, which are always denied, and struggles, which are always international."[153] But not just world literatures, as Casanova argues here, national literatures are also formed by a series of wars of position within the national traditions and innovations. Once this is understood, and even though Casanova does not mention this, it is hard to dismiss the various manipulations of nation-states to control the definition of literature as irrelevant, even if one is agnostic about the loss of autonomy. And while it is painful to say, all these various and often contradictory forms of support create the category of "American literature."

CHAPTER THREE

Stubborn Nationalism

Example Two, Movement Literatures

WHILE WRITING THIS BOOK, I kept thinking about Donald M. Allen's *The New American Poetry*. Mainly I thought about this work because it was through this anthology that I became interested in literature (and in many ways this book is an autobiography about how my education told me that certain forms of literature were autonomous when they were not and how long it took me to realize this). The anthology was an assigned book for at least three classes that I took as an undergraduate (although this has probably more to do with the fact that I got my undergraduate degree at Bard College and took classes there from Ron Loewinsohn—who was teaching at Bard while on leave from UC Berkeley for a year—and Robert Kelly than with end-of-the-twentieth-century pedagogical practices). However, Loewinsohn and Kelly were not alone in seeing it as a game-changing anthology. Many have presented Allen's anthology as prescient, foreseeing the changing mores of how we understand U.S. literature. Perloff in "Whose New American Poetry? Anthologizing in the Nineties" traces the impact of *The New American Poetry* in some detail.[1] Jed Rasula locates his version of what I am calling the two traditions of modernism and New Criticism in a "battle" between the Allen anthology and the Donald Hall, Robert Pack, and Louis Simpson anthology, *New Poets of England and America*. He writes, "The habitual and often gratuitous mention of this 'battle' has permeated the study of American poetry in the last thirty years—so much so that it would be fair to think of it as a perpetual *rerun* much like a syndicated television program."[2]

It is not just that this story is on constant repeat. *The New American Poetry* was presented as the progressive alternative in the classes that I took at Bard. And this is one possible example of state and foundation networks reframing modernism. First published in 1960 by Grove Press, *The New American Poetry* is in many ways closer to the legacy of *Perspectives USA* than it is to say Jolas's *Transition*. For *The New American Poetry*, with its "American" modifier, makes an argument for modernism as an American tradition, not an internationalist one, and one that is more concerned with aesthetics. It became, as Barnhisel puts it when discussing Laughlin's editing of *Perspectives USA*, "used to defend the very societies and political *systems* toward which much Modernist art had been, and still was, so relentlessly hostile."[3] There is not, as with Laughlin's editing of *Perspectives USA*, any evidence that Hall's anthology had a deliberate soft diplomatic or nationalist agenda, that he wanted it to defeat leftist intellectuals in dialectical combat. But *The New American Poetry* comes out of the same Cold War literary scene. Similar to Laughlin, Barney Rosset, the editor of Grove Press, worked with UNESCO in the 1950s, and as Loren Glass points out in *Counterculture Colophon*, these ties shaped Grove early on as a publisher of international literature. Glass also mentions that Allen was "Rosset's key partner" for finding the latest in European avant-garde literature.[4] (Another interesting anecdote from Glass's study is that Rosset set up a prize to reward literature written in English in India so as to further cultural relations between the United States and India, a move right out of the Congress for Cultural Freedom playbook.) But while there is no suggestion of *The New American Poetry* being funded by the synergies I have been charting between the state and private foundations, as with many things, nationalism is not only something bought, it is something that many participate in voluntarily and something that is passively affirmed. One of my presumptions here is that the relentless attention that the state and private foundations gave to cultural production of all sorts dramatically altered U.S. literary production. It set something in motion.

The New American Poetry collects the work of a number of poets, most not previously anthologized and a number of whom would become prominent in the U.S. poetry scene following the anthology's publication. As it does this, it divides the poets into somewhat idiosyncratic aesthetic categories that use a sort of city-state grouping: Black Mountain, San Francisco Renaissance, New York Poets, Beat Generation, and a fifth group without geographical definition. The poems included in *The New American Poetry* are formally modernist. Or as Allen writes, "one common characteristic: a total rejection of all those qualities typical of academic verse. Following the practice and precepts of Ezra Pound and William Carlos Williams, it has built on their achievements and gone on to evolve new conceptions of the poem. These poets have already created their own tradition, their own press, and their public. They are our avant-garde, the true continuers of the modern movement in American poetry."[5] He is right. The poets in *The New American Poetry* are the continuers of modernism, of a sort of national American modernism. His locating this legacy in Pound (the anti-Semitic supporter of fascism) and Williams ("All I want to do is to state that poetry, in its sources, body, spirit, in its form, in short, is related to poetry and not to socialism, communism, or anything else that tries to swallow it.") is telling.[6] While there are a few exceptions, the New American poets tend to stay home, their poems tend to be located in the United States, and, especially when compared to avant garde modernism, are notably monolingual. There are around three poets out of the forty-four included in the anthology that attempt to represent something other than a U.S. landscape, include languages other than English, or attempt to think about global culture (rather than national culture): Charles Olson (in "the Kingfishers"), Robert Duncan (in "The Question" and "A Poem Beginning with a Line by Pindar"), and Frank O'Hara (in "In Memory of My Feelings" and "Ode: Salute to the French Negro Poets"). This does not make the work nationalist necessarily, but internationalism, and with it the inclusion of other national languages and the attention to dialects and creoles and idiolects that were central to much of avant garde modernist work, is barely present in this work.

The story of the divide between modernist and New Critical traditions got it half right and half wrong, and so Allen was half right and half wrong. He was right about the decentralization, that by mid-century there was no longer a single American Literary Tradition, only a dissimulating claim to this title by those continuing in the New Critical tradition. Right about how there were many smaller, specific, and often competing literary cultures. All of this would have been hard to miss. But his racialized and gendered emphasis—he includes one (male) who identifies as other than white and four white women—meant that he missed the most influential and powerful form that this decentralization took: how many writers at this time instead of writing a literature of presumed universalism, wrote literatures that were allied with and written for and about various specific racial and cultural and political communities, not for America as a whole and not about Americans as a whole. Smethurst in *The Black Arts Movement,* for instance, puzzles over the large number of African American writers in the scene that are not included in *The New American Poetry:* "the New American Poetry was, like the first wave of Modernism, considerably less 'white' than has often been advertised and a decisive influence on later nationalist literary movements."[7] He also notices that "despite a general sense of being in conflict with McCarthyism, virtually none of these poets (even those, such as Ginsberg, Kaufman, and Perkoff, who had once had some direct ties to the CPUSA and the Popular Front) retained any significant organizational connection to the remaining institutions of the Communist left much into the 1950s; they were, in fact, generally hostile or indifferent to the Soviet Union and to the remnants of the Communist movement in the United States."[8] And reading Smethurst's very detailed historical accounting of the socialities of the period one is left with the sense of how inadequate *New American Poetry* is to the time. That Allen did not include the most direct predecessors for this sort of work—the many leftist writers who were part of the popular front aesthetics—in his anthology ends up almost saying something very similar to what Laughlin was saying with *Perspectives USA:* that "new" American poetry (or U.S. writing in the tradition of modernism) was not resistant, that it was amenable to literary nationalism.

The conditions that would eventually produce the many literatures that were aligned with, created by, or nurtured by various culturalist movements was already in formation in 1960, but they were solidified when Malcolm X was shot (five years after the publication of *The New American Poetry*). That event more than any other heralded the arrival of movement literature. Amiri Baraka puts it like this in "The Black Arts (Harlem, Politics, Search for a New Life)": "When Malcolm was murdered we felt that was the final open declaration of war on black people and we resolved to fight. The Harlem move was our open commitment to this idea. In our naïve and subjective way we fully expected the revolution to jump off any minute."[9]

Baraka's claim that the expectation of revolution was naïve and subjective though might have been at the time less naïve and subjective. As Max Elbaum notes in *Revolution in the Air*, by early 1971 "tens of thousands believed revolution was not only desirable, but also possible—and maybe even not too far around the corner."[10] And it matters to understandings of this literature that it was founded in a moment when it looked as if a major national uprising could happen. There were major rebellions across the United States starting in the mid-1960s and continuing into the 1970s. Major uprisings and riots took place at the start of 1964 in Rochester, Philadelphia, Harlem, Chicago, Jersey City, Paterson, and Elizabeth; then, Watts in 1965; Cleveland in 1966; Newark, Detroit, and Minneapolis-St. Paul in 1967; Chicago, Baltimore, Washington DC, and Cleveland in 1968. Many sources attribute over 150 various rebellions in 1967; over 125 after the shooting of Martin Luther King Jr. in 1968.[11] Politicized bombings were a regular occurrence: there were over 4,000 in the United States between January 1969 and April 1970. And there was an emerging organized leftism. There were significant numbers of strikes in

1960 and 1970. The largest wildcat strike in U.S. history happened in 1970 when federal postal workers struck in March. The New Communist Movement, while made up of many very localized splinter groups, was huge and some estimate that it had close to 10,000 core activists.[12]

The relation between these political movements and movement literature of the late 1960s and early 1970s was often fairly direct. As Loren Glass observed in *Counterculture Colophon,* "To be in the Movement meant, at least partly, to be reading certain books."[13] And many leftist movements at the time had a special interest in the arts as a place that can represent and preserve cultures and their values, as a place that is ideal for political education and debate. An interest in "cultural independence," in "revolutionary culture," in the arts and the role of arts in education, for instance, shows up again and again in the political communiqués from this period. "El Plan Espiritual de Aztlán," often considered among the foundational declarations of Chicano/a nationalism, proclaims, "Once we are committed to the idea and philosophy of El Plan de Aztlán, we can only conclude that social, economic, cultural, and political independence is the only road to total liberation from oppression, exploitation, and racism. Our struggle then must be for the control of our barrios, campos, pueblos, lands, our economy, our culture, and our political life. El Plan commits all levels of Chicano society—the barrio, the campo, the ranchero, the writer, the teacher, the worker, the professional—to La Causa."[14] The "13 Point Program and Platform" of the Young Lords includes a demand for "a true education of our Creole culture and Spanish language. We must learn our history of fighting against cultural, as well as economic genocide by the yanqui. Revolutionary culture, culture of our people, is the only true teaching."[15] Even "the Black Panther Party for Self-

Defense Ten-Point Platform and Program" includes a statement of belief in "an educational system that will give our people a knowledge of self. If a man does not have knowledge of himself and his position in society and the world, then he has little chance to relate to anything else."[16] (Even as various Panthers were at best hesitant and often openly hostile to the idea that culture is a meaningful part of liberation struggles; see, for instance, Linda Harrison's "On Cultural Nationalism."[17]) And a series of loosely organized cultural centers and affiliations emerged *from* various political organizations (not the reverse; this is an important distinction that people who are optimistic about the relationship between literature and protest often miss). Umbra, a collective of mainly black poets, was founded a few years before, in 1962. It developed out of On Guard for Freedom, an organization that in 1961 led a fairly intense demonstration at the UN to protest the murder of Patrice Lumumba. In "The Wailer" Baraka writes of meeting Askia Toure "fighting police while protesting Lumumba's murder."[18] In 1965 El Teatro Campesino was founded on the Delano Grape Strike picket lines of Cesar Chavez's United Farmworkers. And not just organizations. Individuals also became writers because of their involvement in these movements. John Trudell often credits his activism for his turn to poetry. Alurista is so tied into the origins of Chicano nationalism that his writing opens the "El Plan Espiritual de Aztlán" and the 1969 National Youth Liberation Conference where this manifesto was written was organized by the poet Rodolfo "Corky" Gonzales.

It is obvious when reading the literatures of these various movements of the late 1960s and early 1970s that they had learned from the role literature (and anticolonial language preservation movements) played in decolonization. Much of this literature, with its calls for both resistance and cultural uplift, is more philosophically aligned with the work in journals such as *Présence Africaine* than with the more nationally representative American literatures. Baraka begins his essay "The Black Arts (Harlem, Politics, Search for a New Life)" with the declaration that "the arrival uptown, Harlem, can only be summed up by the feelings jumping out of Césaire's *Return to My Native Land* or Fanon's *The Wretched of the Earth* or Cabral's *Return to the Source*."[19] He continues, "The emergence of the independent African states and the appearance of African freedom fighters, fighting guerilla wars with white colonialism, was destined to produce young intellectuals (and older ones too) who reveled in the spirit of defiant revolution and sought to use it to create art."[20]

Gonzales's *I Am Joaquin* is among the more interesting and often overlooked works to come out of this period. *I Am Joaquin* was first published in 1967 by Crusade for Justice, the Denver area community-based organization that Gonzales founded. Like *Tender Buttons, I Am Joaquin* has unpretentious beginnings. It was published first as a cheaply printed, stapled pamphlet. But beyond that, it is a very different poem, written in a different time for very different reasons. It is a list poem about Chicano identity (women show up in it but it is primarily a poem about male identity, about Joaquin; perhaps one could generously read it as the gendered generic). Anzaldúa notices its importance: "Chicanos did not know we were a people until 1965 when Cesar Chavez and the farmworkers united and *I Am Joaquín* was published and *la Raza Unida* party was formed in Texas."[21] And while it lacks the internationalism of avant garde modernism, it is transnational with its attention to how Chicano identity is formed at the border between Mexico and the United States. Gonzales writes it in a Spanish-inflected English so it is an important predecessor to the work that so interests me in the 1990s. In its 1967 edition it also appears with a Spanish translation. So it pointedly circulates in two languages, although with the telling peculiarity that the two languages are not evenly represented in that it is written in English and then this English is mixed with Spanish but the Spanish translation is just in Spanish and does not include English. The poem is a sort of persona poem and it begins with Joaquin confessing that he is "caught up in a whirl of an gringo society" and his cure for that, he states, is to "withdraw to the safety within the circle of life . . . / MY OWN PEOPLE."[22] But Joaquin's people, as he points out, are multivalent and Gonzales's Joaquin is many things, mainly many Latina and Latino things. He is Cuauhtémoc and Nezahualcoyotl; he rides with Don Benito Juarez and Pancho Villa; he is "the black shawled / faithful women"; he is "Aztec Prince and Christian Christ."[23]

Formally, the poem is a cataloguing list. And with its length and its stirring rhythmic incantations and inclusive (even if separatist) cultural politics, it is clearly not conventional lyric. The Bantam edition of the poem (which has a lot of unattributed ancillary material) in a section called "About I am Joaquín" also states: "The poem was written first and foremost for the Chicano movement."[24] What this means is that the poem's reason for being was to support struggles over things like access to land and education, to support workers' rights, and to stir the emotions that lead to resistance. Rafael Pérez-Torres notes that I Am Joaquin is a poem that was written as "an organizing tool": "Written in 1967 for the Crusade for Justice, distributed by mimeographed copy, recited at rallies and strikes, the poem functions within a system of economic and political resistance."[25]

There are many provocative aesthetic and formal moves that Gonzales uses to write a poem for a movement. One is that he uses a singular individual to articulate a collective, but pointedly not personal, identity. That it is not universal (the poem does not say that Joaquin is all humans; Joaquin is clearly not a part of "gringo society") does not discount its attention to collectivity; it rather is one of the ways the poem points to how uneven development is counter-collective. Another is his decision to write that collectivity with more than one national language. And yet another is that he reconfigures a long literary tradition, one that has historically vacillated between being nationalist and resistant. Gonzales did not invent the "I am . . ." poem. It has long been a nationalist form. Walt Whitman is, obviously, a founding father of this sort of poem. In Whitman's hands the statement of identity is an articulation of an inclusive U.S. national identity. The "I" of "Song of Myself," for instance, claims many identities: "I am the hounded slave"; "I am an old artillerist"; "I am the mash'd fireman with breast-bone broken."[26] Gonzales's decision to use a Whitmanesque form to delineate an identity that is culturally separatist (as in Chicano only) yet inclusive in what gets included in the category of Chicano (his inclusiveness is, of course, transnational in the same way that the term "Chicano" is a transnational subjectivity) was not without precedent. It is similar to Hughes's use of the same form to also articulate the possibility of a separatist and yet inclusive and pointedly not national identity in much of his work. "Negro," for instance, begins "I am a Negro" and then goes through a series of different qualifying identities such as slave, worker, singer, victim. In "Let America Be America Again," Hughes is even more inclusive: "I am the poor white, fooled and pushed apart, / I am the Negro bearing slavery's scars. / I am the red man driven from the land, / I am the immigrant clutching the hope I seek—."[27]

   I Am Joaquin obviously exemplifies how many associated with more militant movements thought of literature as possibly being a meaningful tool for organizing. But also its publication history is indicative of how many at the time cultivated decentralized and community based support structures so that this literature might exist. This conviction was in no way an idea that was unique to Crusade for Justice. Many political groups and the writers affiliated with them at the time developed similar publication and distribution infrastructures. And many writers felt it was important to support these emerging networks with their work; even someone as established as Gwendolyn Brooks. In the 1950s, Brooks was one of few black poets recognized by Official Verse Culture. She had published a number of books with Harper & Row and she won the Pulitzer Prize in 1950. (Or somewhat recognized; an often-told story has Wallace Stevens when he saw a photograph of Brooks in 1952 remarking "Who's the coon?"[28]) Then she attended the second Fisk Black Writers Conference in 1967. "In 1967," John K. Young writes in *Black Writers, White Publishers,* "Gwendolyn Brooks famously became a black nationalist poet."[29] Brooks describes this moment much more modestly in *Report from Part One* as the moment of arriving to "a surprised queenhood in the new black sun," a moment that qualified her to "enter at least the kindergarten of new consciousness now. New consciousness and trudge-toward-progress."[30] Whatever one calls it, after 1967, she left Harper & Row. Brooks repeatedly said that she did not leave her publisher because she had a complaint with them (several times in interviews she calls it the "Harper harbor"), but because she wanted to support black publishing: "I have left Harper not because of any difficulty therewith, but simply because my first duty is to the estimable, developing black publishing companies."[31]

Riot was her first publication after this decision. And just as I think recognizing that *I Am Joaquin* is a crucial work I want to argue this about *Riot* too (that both are also, along with *Tender Buttons,* self-, friend-, or community-published pamphlets is at the least interesting and perhaps another indication of how important it is to maintain independent venues for publication). It seems telling that Brooks's first poem after leaving Harper & Row opens with the possible death of a white man and is supportive of the riots in Chicago that took place after the assassination of Martin Luther King Jr. It was published in 1969 by Broadside Press, which was run by Dudley Randall out of his home and was in the process of becoming one of the most significant publishers of black poetry. In an article that muddies the differences between "cultural capital" and actual capital, James Sullivan calls this decision to leave Harper & Row for Broadside a "profoundly anti-economic move."[32] I would want to see some sales numbers to figure out the actual economics of this move. There is much to suggest that Broadside titles sold as well as those published by more established New York publishing houses. Haki R. Madhubuti, writing then under the name Don L. Lee, notes that "Harper's never, and I mean that literally, pushed the work of Gwendolyn Brooks."[33] And Sonia Sanchez claims that titles on Broadside Press sold "more than one hundred thousand copies of our books in our time"; that "we were able to sell hundreds of thousands of copies of our poems."[34] She might be exaggerating (although maybe not if by "we" she means all Broadside Press authors). But even if her numbers seem high, it was a time when a small press could have a substantial impact. It is also probably important to note here that the publishing industry was beginning to consolidate into various multinational corporations and as it did this it would become less defined by cultural capital and more interested in actual capital. This would result in firms such as Harper & Row publishing much less literature, especially poetry. And in a pattern that continues to define contemporary literary production, small presses, such as Broadside, would do more and more of this work. But I am also not sure that the economics of it matter that much. What matters is that it mattered to Brooks and a bunch of other writers at the time that their work be distributed by politicized and community attentive presses, that it be autonomous from dominant publication and distribution networks.

Riot is a beautiful book, one in which every design decision feels loaded with accusation. There is a black first page with a Henry Miller quote from *Sunday After the War* in white type: "It would be a terrible thing for Chicago if this black fountain of life should suddenly erupt. My friend assures me there's no danger of that. I don't feel so sure about it. Maybe he's right. Maybe the Negro will always be our friend, no matter what we do to him."[35] On the flip side of this, there is a return to a white page and on this page is an image by Jeff Donaldson. The painting shows two figures, one holding a figurative wooden sculpture, hands pressed against glass (the glass here represented literally by the word "glass"). It is hard to tell if the sculpture will be used for some window breaking or not but it is a possible reading. Donaldson was one of the founders of AfriCOBRA (African Commune of Bad Relevant Artists), a collective of artists that was formed in 1968 with a commitment to "the collective exploration, development, and perpetuation of an approach to image making which would reflect and project the moods, attitudes, and sensibilities of African Americans independent of the technical and aesthetic strictures of Euro-centric modalities."[36]

Brooks's *Riot* is in three parts: "Riot," "The Third Sermon on the Warpland," and "An Aspect of Love, Alice in the Ice and Fire." The first part tells the story of one "John Cabot," "all whitebluerose below his golden hair."[37] He is repulsed by the riot that seems to be coming to kill him. He might die at the end: "John Cabot went down in the smoke and fire / and broken glass and blood."[38] This is a revisionary, and perhaps even aspirational, history; although eleven people died in the riots, all were black. There does not seem to be an actual "John Cabot" that Brooks was referring to but the surname Cabot is loaded with the very publication histories that Brooks was attempting to avoid. It is the name of an original Boston Brahmin, about whose family it is famously said, *and this is good old Boston, the home of the bean and the cod, where the Lowells talk only to Cabots, and the Cabots talk only to God.* The Lowells will eventually include the poet Robert (who played a significant role in Cold War CIA literary networks). The East Coast publishing industry is endlessly entwined with this old money / new world milieu and it would be this that Brooks left when she turned to Broadside, and later Third World Press, to publish her books. The sermon that follows this section is subtitled "Phoenix" perhaps (the typography requires interpretation). It opens with the pastoral, lyric: "The earth is a beautiful place. / Watermirrors and things to be reflected. / Goldenrod across the little lagoon."[39] This poem, the longest in this short book, juxtaposes different thoughts about riots from figures such as a child, newspaper accounts, "Black Philosopher," "White Philosopher," and others. And then the book ends with a love poem, with a lover invoking a beloved, that is resolved in a final "we": "We go / in different directions / down the imperturbable street."[40]

There are many arguments yet to be made about the importance of these movement associated literatures. Although these various literatures have received and continue to receive a significant amount of scholarly attention, I am convinced that the aggregate impact of this literature remains underrecognized. If scholars considered movement literature as a whole, rather than as a series of racially segregated subcategories such as Black Arts and Nuyorican and so on, it would be the dominant U.S. literary tradition in the last half of the twentieth century. These literatures of the late 1960s and early 1970s very literally change the map. If one can think of early twentieth-century literature as defined by a standoff between the nationalist New Criticism and the internationalist modernism, after mid-century the idea of only two traditions is no longer in any way representative. This is true despite how this story of two traditions remains powerfully defining to many still today. Some of the defenses of this opposition as the only opposition are by parties who stand to benefit from maintaining it. (Silliman's allegiance to this opposition would be one example of this.) But even scholars who look beyond official verse culture have tended to conceive of U.S. literature as having a dominant, official tradition and then a series of small independent publishing and distribution networks that support work that is about and written from various distinctive cultural and racial traditions. Scholarly study after scholarly study presents these literatures as marginal. However, the term "dominant" in this time is less descriptive of the aesthetic tendencies, readership, or critical attention that a sociologist, or a follower of Moretti or Pierre Bourdieu, might use to determine the "dominant" literatures of the 1960s and 1970s and more descriptive of who controls the spoils, such as the academic jobs.

In short, the moment that produced not only Gonzales's *I Am Joaquin* and Brooks's *Riot* is a moment when a more militant politics put a certain pressure on U.S. literary production and out of this pressure came works that were calls for revolution that challenged racialized and gendered universalism, were frequently contestatory towards capitalism, and refused accommodationist inclusions. It is a moment with a lot of reach. It will lead even Maya Angelou (who began her career touring for the U.S. State Department production of *Porgy and Bess* and thus as part of the U.S. anticommunist cultural diplomacy machine, and ended it as an inaugural poet) to write work such as "Riot: 1960s," a poem that juxtaposes "Hospitality, southern-style" with "lootin' n burnin'" and then police murder: "national guard nervous with his shiny gun / goose the moter quicker / here's my nigga picka / shoot him in the belly / shoot him while he run."[41]

But this moment is short-lived. Most of the more militant cultural centers do not last more than a few years. The Black Arts Repertory Theatre / School did not make it a year. The New Lafayette Theatre, Umbra, and the Watts Writers Workshop did not last much into the 1970s. And by the end of the century, things were different. One way to notice it is in the "I am . . ." poem, which had morphed from the militant separatism of *I Am Joaquin* to something like "the essay in assimilation" that is Marilyn Chin's "How I Got That Name."[42] Or another way of putting this: movement literature with its ties to militant resistance morphed into multicultural literature; into concerns about representation and inclusion. Chin's poem begins "I am Marilyn Mei Ling Chin" and much of the poem is about how the larger forces of assimilation impact her personally and without her consent. It is her father who is the

paperson
who in the late 1950s
obsessed with a bombshell blond
transliterated "Mei Ling" to "Marilyn."[43]

To notice that Chin's poem is about assimilation not resistance is not a complaint about Chin's poem. As the poem's subtitle—"an essay on assimilation"—indicates, her poem is more about the change I am noticing rather than an unreflective perpetuation of it. Chin is writing in the way that one writes when one writes out of movement literature's traditions but thirty years later and as a writer supported by the academy and not by a cultural nationalist movement. There is a poignant awareness of this in her poem; an ironic distance can be read into lines such as

> Oh, how I love the resoluteness
> of that first person singular
> followed by that stalwart indicative
> of "be," without the uncertain i-n-g
> of "becoming."[44]

My argument is not Gonzales good, Chin bad. Instead I have questions that are this book's reason for existing: why did this happen?; how did the separatism of Gonzales's *I Am Joaquin* morph into the study of assimilation that is Chin's "How I Got That Name"?; and what does this tell us about literature's possible relationship to resistance?

There are a number of possible reasons as to why literature stopped being such a crucial part of the resistance movements of the late 1960s and early 1970s. To blame it entirely on the continuing resonances of government and foundation manipulation would be too simplistic. Gentrification, for instance, put the social centers and theaters and other sorts of semipublic or public spaces that often supported this work at risk. A quick summary of a much more complicated momentum: as it is the existence of working-class neighborhoods (created by an urban industrial base) that created the social centers that ended up cultivating urban resistant movements and their literatures in the 1970s, these same urban areas were defined at the end of the century less by white flight and more by gentrification as the demographic of mainly white middle-class workers who had previously moved to the suburbs returned to urban areas. Those who study gentrification in more detail give many reasons for this. Among them is that the same post-1973 economic precarity that radicalized these urban working class communities also eventually demolished them. Urban manufacturing in the United States declined after the 1970s. This meant that working class people lost employment opportunities and thus the reason to live in the city. At the same time, more women entered the work force in an attempt to counter declining buying power. Because the nuclear family no longer had a presumed stay-at-home parent, middle-class families were motivated to move back into urban areas so their homes could be near their jobs. This is the story of white flight turning into gentrification. And as many have noted, this is a large and complicated story with a lot of Machiavellian players. But the result is that the community centers that were petri dishes for resistance movements and their literatures were unable to afford the higher rents that resulted from gentrification. And at the same time, the culturally specific working class community that they represented no longer resided in the neighborhood.

Still, it would be naïve to naturalize the decline of movement literature solely on economic changes or changing cultural concerns, for by the 1960s and 1970s the U.S. government and foundation networks that created the extended reach of the Congress for Cultural Freedom were robust, despite the dissolution of the congress. The story from here on out will have the government supporting with one hand and taking away with the other. It might make sense though to begin this U.S.-focused story with the American Society of African Culture, or to begin it in 1959 when the congress was still functioning. The American Society of African Culture was the U.S. branch of the Société Africaine de Culture, the organization that was created after the *Présence Africaine* conferences. Wilford calls the society "the CIA's principal front organization in the African American literary community."[45] As such, the society did what CIA associated organizations tend to do. They organized conferences, such as the 1959 First Conference of Negro Writers. They organized lecture series. They published books. They funded "annual conferences, festivals in Africa, book publications, and expenses-paid travels to African and Europe."[46] And they turned those who participated in their programming into an extended network. They not only often required reports from those they sent abroad, but staff members were also required to meet regularly with handlers.[47] They sent James Farmer, founder of the Congress of Racial Equity, on a five-week tour of Africa to counter "what has been said in Africa by such 'spokesmen' as Malcolm X."[48] They opened a branch in Lagos to extend their reach into Africa. And they worked with the Senegalese government and UNESCO to organize the First World Festival of Negro Arts. And all of this was happening, as Mary Helen Washington documents in *The Other Blacklist,* at a time when "institutions that had supported black left-wing cultural production has been decimated through all sorts of Red Scare tactics, chief among them being named to the Attorney General's List of Subversive Organizations (AGSLOSO), a totally arbitrary list that allowed the attorney general to declare an organization suspect without any legal proceedings. One of the most effective and innovative leftist cultural organizations in the 1950s, the Committee for the Negro in the Arts, was dead in three months after being designated 'subversive' by the AGLOSO."[49]

By the late 1960s and early 1970s, the U.S. government through COINTELPRO harassed the members of the various movements associated with the ongoing insurgency in the United States and also associated cultural centers. The harassment of cultural centers associated with late 1960s and 1970s movements was at moments fairly intense. The Watts Writers Workshop, for instance, was burned down in 1973 by FBI informant Darthard Perry.[50] The story behind Perry's burning of the Watts Writers Workshop is probably not yet fully told and might never be completely understood (the FBI claims he acted on his own, but whether this is true or not, Perry would not have been hanging around the Watts Writers Workshop if the FBI had not been paying him to be there). At other moments it was likely more volunteeristic. Juan Felipe Herrera tells the story of how the Mission Cultural Center was taken over by a reactionary who, according to Gato Murguía, denounced various left writers to the State Department and then, when a number of poets went to Central America to support the Sandinistas and thus were not around to protest, announced he was "expelling politics from the Mission Cultural Center."[51] The FBI targeted black writers in particular during the late 1960s and 1970s for relentless monitoring. William J. Maxwell, for instance, compiled a list of significant black writers drawing on publication records and anthologies such as the *Norton*. A full 48 percent of the writers on his list of significant black writers were monitored, a number that is disproportionately high in comparison to white American writers that the state had monitored over the years.[52] This monitoring was never entirely clandestine, nor does it seem like the FBI wanted it to be. The FBI files that

Maxwell posted online show the FBI deliberately making their presence known by approaching their subjects for "questioning" again and again. When it comes to COINTELPRO, as far as it is understood now, the harassment of writers involved in these movements and the literary institutions created by these movements to support them was more tepid than anything else. Unlike say Fred Hampton, no one got murdered. But still it is probably just as important not to dismiss observations that the goal of that monitoring, as of the murdering too, was to discourage future action, discourage writers and others from supporting the possible armed militancy that seemed to be emerging from many of these movements. Often writers and literary institutions were subject to monitoring and recuperation at the same time. This has frequently bewildered both the recipients of this sort of attention and literary scholars. Whitney, for instance, calls the way the CIA both funneled money and monitored Baldwin and Wright "positively schizophrenic."[53] But once the money is understood not as support or reward but as co-optation then the funding and the monitoring make more sense. The story of Black Arts Repertory Theatre/School is telling, as it received both federal funds and FBI agents sitting in on its classes.

Basically, just as certain forms of cultural nationalism had their own literatures and support systems for these literatures, fear of militancy—a fear that was provoked by the riots and bombings and occupations that happened in the late 1960s to early 1970s—guided U.S. social policy in the years that followed. It led to a well-funded and powerful counterinsurgency as foundations worked with the U.S. government to fund a mainstream artistic multiculturalism along with a number of economic development initiatives, university area studies programs, changes to school curricula, and other programs. As early as 1971, Frances Fox

Piven and Richard A. Cloward in *Regulating the Poor* noted that it was militancy that lead to increases in social services and grants, not need.[54] (There is some obvious irony in that more insurgent forms of protest that create liberal reforms are decried by those who want liberal reforms. And the reverse too. Those who most want insurgency end up provoking a series of liberal co-optive reforms.) Joan Roelofs in *Foundations and Public Policy* also notices that "to perform its hegemonic role, foundations must absorb rising social power and allow the attainment of real benefits, while diverting systemic challenges."[55]

The history of foundations rushing in to support culture so as to mollify various uprisings has a long history in the United States. The summer of 1919, for instance, was defined by a number of uprisings in which black residents fought back against various forms of white mob violence, most astoundingly in Chicago, but also in more than thirty other towns and cities including Philadelphia, Knoxville, Memphis, New York City, and Baltimore. In response an extended grant system emerged that focused on black cultural production. Among the foundations involved were the Harmon, the Rosenwald, the Phelps-Stokes, the Rockefeller, and the Carnegie Foundations. Some of these foundations refocused their mission to support black cultural production. The Harmon Foundation, established in 1922 to support the building of playgrounds and nursing education, switched its focus to black cultural production in 1925 and gave significant awards in eight fields: business, education, fine arts, literature, music, race relations, religious service, and science. Others narrowed their focus so as create various specific sorts of cultural production. The Rosenwald Fund, established in 1917 by Sears magnate Julius Rosenwald, ran an extensive fellowship program for "Negroes of unusual talent and ability" and "white Southerners" to write a novel about race.

Almost two-thirds of its fellowships during this period went to black writers including James Weldon Johnson, Langston Hughes, and Claude McKay.

In that moment, some writers, both those who received funds and those who did not, worried about this funding from private foundations. Some complained about being forced to write the race novel. Richard Gibson in "A No to Nothing" opens with a story of a (presumed white) publisher who is only willing to publish the race novel and argues that this system "might help account for the monotony and mediocrity of much that parades as 'Negro Literature.'"[56] Some recognized its uselessness to significant structural change. Hughes's famous declaration that "the ordinary Negroes hadn't heard of the Negro Renaissance. And if they had, it hadn't raised their wages any" is but one example.[57] Others worried about its co-optation. Chester Himes in "The Dilemma of the Negro Novelist in U.S." notices how "the appeal to retrench, equivocate, compromise, will be issued by friend and foe alike. The temptations to accede will be tempting, the rewards coercive. The oppressor pays, and sometimes well, for the submission of the oppressed."[58] Others worried about its misdirection and how cultural progress might happen at the expense of and cover over the need for meaningful socioeconomic reform. Arthur Fauset saw a "socio-political-economic setback" because of the dissimulating belief at the time that significant economic reform would come "once the race has produced a sufficiently large number of persons who have properly qualified themselves in the arts."[59]

There is a robust scholarship around 1919 and the years after it about whether to understand the culturalist turn as defusing the resistance of the time or as an aligned insurgency. Barbara Foley does an excellent job of summarizing this debate in *Spectres of*

1919. She points to scholars such as Ann Douglas who argues that "black art engendered followings that sometimes doubled as constituencies, lobbies, and even armies.[60] And on the other side, scholars who argue that cultural production was aligned not with the insurgency but with the repression of the insurgency. David Levering Lewis, for instance: "The Red Summer of 1919, a period of socialist agitation and conservative backlash following the Russian Revolution, produced the trauma that led to the cultural sublimation of civil rights."[61] And Nathan Irvin Huggins in his study *Harlem Renaissance* argues that even though a number of militant poems—such as McKay's "If We Must Die"—were written in the era, those who argued that cultural production was an important site of resistance had "naïve assumptions about the centrality of culture, unrelated to economic and social realities."[62] And also that "black intellectuals seemed unprepared for that rude shock which was to make their paeans to black art and identity echo false."[63] Jodi Melamed points out how the protest novel, not just the race novel that Rosenwald funded but also liberal multicultural literature of the last half of the century, was instrumentalized so as neutralize critical antiracism. In her formulation, literature represented so as to destroy. Foley herself provides some useful nuance to Douglas and others who see culture as a de facto meaningful part of resistance when she notices that "the production of literature inflected with revolutionary politics had slowed to a near-trickle by the last half of the decade."[64] And she also notices how "by the late 1920s, McKay had ceased penning class-conscious poetry and had taken to writing novels bathed in primitivist premises" and also that "Hughes wrote few revolutionary poems between 1926 and kept radical social analysis under careful wraps in *Not without Laughter.*"[65] Foley's study, as nuanced as it is on the various forms of political repression that defined the era, does not spend much time on the possibility that a significant influx of foundation funding might have played a role in severing writers from the mass proletarian movement that defined 1919 (even though it seems in some ways an obvious question to consider as funding for writers coincided with a significant repression of the insurgent workers movement).

Just as in 1919, so in the late 1960s and early 1970s. The Ford Foundation, for instance, in direct response to the hot summers of the 1960s and 1970s, put $100 million into various militancy-quelling projects from 1965 to 1969 and eventually by 1970 devoted 40 percent of its budget to "rights for minorities."[66] Karen Ferguson in *Top Down: The Ford Foundation, Black Power, and the Reinvention of a Radical Liberalism* tells a series of stories about the Ford Foundation's creation of community theaters to showcase more accommodationist work that encouraged assimilation into mainstream U.S. culture rather than the revolutionary resistance that cultural nationalist theaters were so powerfully articulating at the time. Ferguson estimates that around seventeen theaters were directly founded or taken over by the Ford Foundation for this purpose. But the scope of these programs extended way beyond these seventeen theaters as many not-for-profits were dependent on Ford Foundation funds and the era's only other national arts funders, the Rockefeller Foundation and the National Endowment for the Arts, often made their funds contingent on matching support from the Ford Foundation. She writes, "Between the late 1950s and the early 1970s, the number of nonprofit, professional repertory theaters in the United States rose from barely a handful to around forty, and by 1969 they employed more actors than Broadway did. The Foundation could take most of the credit for this florescence."[67] Roelofs notices something similar, how the National Urban Coalition in 1967 "channeled support and status to moderates and redefined 'black power' as 'black capitalism.'"[68]

No one was more aware of this counter insurgency than Baraka, perhaps because of his experience with Black Arts Repertory Theatre / School. The Theatre / School was started late April 1965. That summer the Theatre / School received significant funds from HARYOU-ACT. HARYOU, an antipoverty organization started by Kenneth Clark in 1962, along with several other organizations had received significant federal funding in 1965 to get youth off the streets of Harlem to avert riots. Things were tense. Malcolm X had been shot in February and Harlem had rioted for six days during the previous summer after the New York Police Department shot James Powell, a black fifteen-year-old. The funds were famously misappropriated (there was a plan to plant 1,500 trees in Harlem that summer and apparently only one got planted). But as a riot prevention program it was successful. A number of riots happened in other cities in the summer of 1965, but none in Harlem. After the risk of a hot summer was over, the federal government pulled the funds. So first the Black Arts Repertory Theatre / School was co-opted to do the work of pacification of resistance that Baraka was in some ways committed to cultivating. (Although a caveat here: Baraka's politics were very much in flux throughout his life and he seems to have had no consistent pro- or antiriot position; in "Black Arts" he tells a story of encouraging looting on a loudspeaker during the 1965 power outage; while he was arrested during the Newark riot of 1967, it was not for rioting, and after the riots he joined Anthony Imperiale and denounced the riots as the work of white outside agitators.[69]) Baraka again and again in years after this experience was one of few relentless critics of government and foundation funding. Many times in interviews he noticed how the Ford Foundation destroyed the community theaters that were producing radical plays, which Ferguson charts in such detail. In an interview with Saul Gottlieb, Baraka explained that "the only way they would give me money now would be to do something they can use against black people."[70]

There are countless examples of this sort of manipulative recuperation by state and private foundations. Part of the $100 million that the Ford Foundation allocated for various militancy-quelling projects went into educational initiatives. The same fear of militancy that led to the development of foundation-funded and businessman-run arts organizations modeled on movement literature's community-attentive production models but without its anticapitalist fervor also led to the transformation of U.S. universities. Universities were also having a similar moment of militancy in the 1960s with huge protests and shutdowns. Among the more militant were the protests, strikes, and building occupations calling for more attention to racial diversity and the establishment of Black and Ethnic Studies departments. Students at San Francisco State University began a strike in November of 1968 that lasted until March of 1969. Armed African American students at Cornell University occupied Willard Straight Hall in April 1969. And by the year's end, over 250 protests had happened at colleges and universities across the country. After the Kent State shootings in May 1970, as Kirkpatrick Sale notes, "students at a total of at least 350 institutions went out on strike and 536 schools were shut down completely for some period of time, 51 of them for the entire year."[71]

The Rockefeller and Ford Foundations and the State Department were, of course, there too, with funds to neutralize the resistance. Noliwe Rooks and Fabio Rojas both point to how black campus militancy led the Ford Foundation to put significant funds into Black Studies departments but only into those that were integrationist in intent and not those that were separatist or had ties to black militancy. Many have observed that while numerous Black Studies programs were created as a result of the Ford Foundation monies, it was at the deliberate expense of more radical student demands for things like open enrollment, scholarship monies, and the hiring of significant numbers of black faculty for these programs. The San Francisco State University strike, for instance, made fifteen supposedly nonnegotiable demands for fairly significant changes such as the hiring of seventy full-time faculty, community control of the new departments that was free from administrative interference, open admissions for students who were not white, and the reinstatement of George Mason Murray (the Black Panther minister of education and also a graduate student at SFSU at the time who had been suspended for fiery rhetoric).[72] When the strike was finally over, many called it a success. As Rooks notes, a School of Ethnic Studies was established and it housed a Department of Black Studies, but the original demands for seventy full-time faculty, for community control, for open admissions, and for Murray's reinstatement were not met. And the drama did not end when the strike ended: "On March 3, 1970, almost a year after the day of the strike's end, [Hayakawa] fired the entire Black Studies faculty, ostensibly because the department had not submitted its hiring, retention, and tenure committee reports until an hour before the deadline."[73] And the School of Ethnic Studies at San Francisco State University, while still operational, remains underfunded and precarious to this day.

But the story that is the establishment of Black Studies in higher education is just one dimension of this especially vexed relationship between higher education and these resistance movements. The 1970s were a unique moment when higher education was a particularly contestatory arena. There were demands for major reforms in higher education, which were first articulated in the context of the militancy that was the San Francisco State University strike and other strikes. These demands were for things such as open admissions (especially for students who did not identify as white only), for community rather than institutional oversight of faculty, and for shifts in hiring and funding priorities toward more black and ethnic studies faculty and programs. If these had been in any way realized, they would have created an entirely different version of higher education. But what was enacted instead was particularly lethal to these demands: an institutionalization of these culturalist movements that would sever them from more insurgent and militant possibilities as they were located within the university. Roderick Ferguson does an excellent job of charting this in *The Reorder of Things* where he looks "at how state, capital, and academy saw minority insurgence as a site of calculation and strategy, how those institutions began to see minority difference and culture as positivities that could be part of their own 'series of aims and objectives.'"[74] And as he notices, "a new mode of biopower—one that affirmed minority difference and culture—would emerge and work with necropolitical social formations to simultaneously activate and disfranchise minoritized subjects and communities, forming and re-forming institutions according to the advancement and regulation of minority difference. If truth be told, institutionalization—for radical social and intellectual movements—was never a simple and innocent cause for celebration. What we find in the history of interdisciplinarity is that incorporation has always been a reason for meditation, scrutiny, and awareness."[75] Melamed calls the resulting canon wars "one kind of counterinsurgency against 1970s social movements," one that made "minoritized difference work for post-Keynesian times—to produce, validate, certify, and affirm racial difference in ways that augmented, enhanced, and developed state-capital hegemony rather than disrupted it."[76]

At the same time, it is not just resistance movements that were institutionalized at the end of the twentieth century. U.S. literary production was as well. More and more writers began to enter higher education to get degrees in creative writing. This relationship between higher education and U.S. literary production has been much studied recently. McGurl in *The Program Era* documents the large impact that higher education had on U.S. literary production throughout the twentieth century. What McGurl calls the Program Era began to percolate after World War II, when over two million veterans went back to school with funding from the G.I. Bill. He mainly tells the story of individual programs (of University of North Carolina, Chapel Hill, Iowa, the famous Stegner workshop) and individual writers (of John Barth, Sandra Cisneros, Flannery O'Connor, Joyce Carol Oates, Philip Roth). He does not address this network of State Department and foundation funding much in *The Program Era*. But just as this sort of funding played a role in directing Black and Latin American studies programs, these networks also funded the development of the discipline of creative writing (although the funding amounts were significantly less). Cultural diplomacy projects such as the State Department's International Writing Program, a program housed at the University of Iowa that funds writers from abroad to come to the United States for workshops and readings were a result of some of this funding. And, as Bennett notices, the Iowa Writers' Workshop (the MFA, not the International Writing Program) also received significant funding from these networks: "The workshop thrived on checks from places like the Rockefeller Foundation, which gave Iowa $40,000 between 1953 and 1956—good money at the time. As the years went by, it also attracted support from the Asia Foundation (another channel for CIA money) and the State Department."[77] His more extended study, *Workshops of Empire*, charts the extent to which "anxieties about totalitarianism, the containment of Communism, the repudiation of American radicalism, the newly powerful mass culture, and the nature of literature all contributed to the contours of the emerging discipline."[78]

I WILL CONTINUE THIS story of creative writing and higher education in the next chapter as it is something that intensifies in the 1990s. But for now, I will end by noting that there is nothing simple in this story of the constant and multivalent recuperation of resistant, other-than-national literatures. It comes from all sides and it works across the private and the public sector. It is amazingly successful. It successfully represses a fairly significant uprising. It successfully utilizes ethnic and racial divisions against equity projects. And it is also successful at remaining under recognized and its fairly profound impact being dismissed. In the next chapter, I describe the national tradition: Standard English literature at the turn of the twenty-first century and its ties to the state and to foundations. The funding that I trace in that chapter is more tepid but no less politicized. It features some new players, and some old ones too.

CHAPTER FOUR

Turn of the Twenty-First Century

The National Tradition

MANY MIGHT ARGUE with my insistence that nationalism (and the particular way it manifests its impact on literature in the United States through a synergy between private foundations and the U.S. government) continues to shape the production of contemporary literature. At the turn of the twenty-first century many assert that the nation-state form is less relevant, that it is a postnational moment. Arjun Appadurai, for instance, in 1996 in *Modernity at Large:* "The nation-state, as a complex modern political form, is on its last legs."[1] And it was not an insane argument in the moment. There were significant shifts in national boundaries at the turn of century. Third world nationalism had lost its revolutionary potential through neocolonial manipulations and there were significant reasons to question the liberatory potential of what is often called liberatory nationalism. Further, all sorts of socioeconomic forces suggested a decline in the power of the nation-state. The Soviet system was collapsing.

(Although the result of this collapse was a rise in nationalism and around twenty-five new nations were formed out of this collapse; this is less than the around sixty-seven that were recognized during the mid-century decolonization movements, but still it is an unusual amount of new nations in comparison to the four or so that were recognized in the 1980s and the three or so that achieved recognition after the 1990s.) The era was defined, as many before me have pointed out, by an intensification of trans-national economic exchanges in which goods and cultures more intensely crossed multiple territories. In the capitalist centers, the finance industry managed to convince many powerful na-tions that they were beholden to it, implying in the process that nation-states were anachronistic, even as multinational flows are so obviously entirely maintained and perpetuated by the militaries of various nation-states. And it was the era of free trade agree-ments. Not just the North American Free Trade Agreement, but also the Canada-U.S. Free Trade Agreement and a whole series of European free trade agreements such as the 1993 Maastricht Treaty, which would eventually lead to the formation of the European Union. Fredric Jameson, from an entirely different pol-itics than Appadurai, in *Postmodernism, or, The Cultural Logic of Late Capitalism* used the term "postmodern hyperspace" to describe these reconfigurations and in the process argued that they impacted economic relations and also could be seen almost mimetically in everything from architecture to literature.[2]

It is true, as Jameson and many other scholars noted this at the time, that a sort of cultural flow shows up in literature at this time that could be seen as mimetic of the economic flows that intensi-fied in the era. And many argued that these representations of transnational cultural exchanges indicated that literature was no longer as stubbornly national as it had been, that this is a global

or worldly or transnational literature instead of a national literature. Most of this scholarship seems oddly optimistic about literature's possible independence from the nation form, while more
or less ignoring that if this were true one of literature's main reasons for existing would be gone (and the significant amount of
funding that comes from the U.S. government that supports literary production, especially "literary fiction" and other prestige
genres with limited sales such as most of poetry, would also dis-
appear). Overlooked by Appadurai—but of course not by
Jameson—is what the many uprisings of the end of the century
made clear: for many, globalization is just another form of imperialism. Appadurai's assertion that it is a postnational era relies
on his observation that technology means that "the United States
is no longer the puppeteer of a world system of images but is only
one node of a complex transnational construction of imaginary
landscapes."[3] It is an odd observation as in 1996, when Appadurai
was writing *Modernity at Large,* the internet was a U.S.-dominated
puppet. The United States in 2016 still published 26 percent of all
books. Also Appadurai seems unable to escape both nationalism
and imperialism in his description of globalization. A few pages
later, his example of this transnational exchange is one that is defined by nations who wield imperial power: "So, while India exports waiters and chauffeurs to Dubai and Sharjah, it also exports
software engineers to the United States—indentured briefly to
Tata-Burroughs or the World Bank, then laundered through the
State Department to become wealthy resident aliens, who are in
turn objects of seductive messages to invest their money and
know-how in federal and state projects in India."[4]

One ramification of these changes, one that I think is not in
argument with Jameson or with Appadurai, is that literature
because of its stubborn relationship to nationalism might not be

the best genre in which to talk about resistance to globalization. While some literature, most of it novels, in this moment suddenly takes global flows and exchanges as part of its form, much of this literature seems more supportive of globalization than critical of it. Further, even if huge economic changes could suggest that nation-states are more interdependent than before (which is about the most optimistic thing I think one can say about the fate of the nation-state during this period), even as literature in response could reflect this by alluding to an array of forms from many different nations, literature would remain influenced by the long history of state manipulation of things literary in a way that it is not by multinational corporations and globalized economic changes. While FedEx, to take a clichéd example of corporate globalization, might donate funds to a nonprofit that supports the arts, it does not have any need to imagine communities (as Anderson phrased it) and so does not bother to directly monitor and harass writers as the governments of nation-states do. Also telling is that the U.S. government and private foundations continued to fund and harass (although there is little evidence that the extremity of monitoring that defined the 1960s and 1970s continues) at the turn of the century, despite, or perhaps because, literature was somewhat more global in its influences and range of references. This might explain why puppets look at the turn of the century like the more autonomous art form. Governments and foundations do not really fund the production of large puppets. And puppets have no stubborn relationship to nationalism.

Basically the specific way that literature is related to the nation-state was underrecognized in scholarly studies of the impact that globalization had on literature prior to the turn of the century and continues to remain underrecognized in the studies of post-45 literatures that were written after the turn of the century. Caren

Irr, for instance, argues that the turn of the century novel is something other than national in *Toward the Geopolitical Novel*. She claims that it "actively seeks creative ways to move beyond existing national forms, and does so because it participates in an active social process in which new political positions and attitudes are emerging."[5] Among her arguments is one about influence, about what sorts of national literary traditions show up in various novels. She points, for instance, to how many of the writers of the geopolitical novel have "spent time in MFA programs in the U.S. and their work may signal 'high cultural pluralism.'"[6] But then she continues that this novel nonetheless is indebted to other traditions, such as "Nigerian popular fiction, the Indian nationalist novel, and Latin American neorealism."[7] Someone less optimistic about such adoptions could call this appropriation. But even if one is more forgiving and calls this influence, it still requires a willful ignoring of the differences between what it means for a genre to be influenced by other forms and what it means to be another genre or form. In other words, the role that the Standard English realist novel has in upholding U.S. nationalism is not necessarily nullified if this form of novel alludes to or appropriates forms from other nations within it.

Also ignored by Irr's study is the large issue that the box that holds these forms is not just the realist novel written in Standard English but this novel is distributed within another box, a publishing industry pursuing the big returns of the large U.S. market. That more and more writers from places where English is newish began to write in Standard English realist novels that are often published and distributed by a multinational publishing industry with a focus on the U.S. market during this time should probably not be read as a diminishment in the power of the United States. It does appear as if there is one major choice for an increasing number of writers from all sorts of nations at the turn of the twenty-first century: to write in Standard English (and mainly to write a realist novel) or to write otherwise. A writer in much of Africa, the Caribbean, and the Pacific has the nonchoice of writing a novel that is formally and linguistically legible to the multinational English (or other imperial language) publishing industry or of attempting to seek publication in a more localized publishing industry with significantly less market share. Many choose the first option. While the largeness of the U.S. publishing market would be one obvious reason to do this, there are some perhaps less obvious (or at least underrecognized by scholars) ones. Since 1967, the U.S. State Department has brought over "fourteen hundred writers from more than 140 countries" to the International Writing Program in Iowa to be trained to write through a series of English language workshops and readings.[8]

There is nothing wrong with this inclusion. I am not arguing that the category of "American literature" should exclude the work of writers who are immigrants or who are not U.S. citizens or that it should not allude or borrow from other cultural traditions. But there are many reasons to be hesitant with any understanding of this as something other than nationalism. Irr's emphasis on literary form means she misses how often this novel has been both used for and shaped by U.S. cultural diplomacy. Many of the writers that she mentions have been found useful for propaganda purposes by the State Department, and especially useful as an example of state-sponsored multiculturalism. Daniel Alarcón, Junot Díaz, and Gary Shteyngart, for instance, are all featured prominently in the State Department propaganda publication called "Multicultural Literature in the United States Today."[9] (This was a publication that was intended to be distributed through U.S. embassies to the elite of various nations of interest.) And a number of other writers of the geopolitical novel have been eager participants in State Department cultural diplomacy programs. Among the writers Irr discusses, a significant number of them—Alarcón, Julia Alvarez, Michael Chabon, Joshua Ferris, Mark Jacobs, Gish Jen, Ha Jin, Shirley Geok-lin Lim, and Bob Shacochis—have read abroad for the State Department, sometimes several times. Others—among them Slavenka Drakulić, Helon Habila, and Victor Pelevin—have been hosted by the State Department as fellows in the International Writing Program. Ha Jin, a Chinese writer who came to the United States for an MFA and stayed, in *The Writer as Migrant* (an excerpt from this book appears in a special issue on muliticultural literature of *eJournalUSA*, one of many publications that the State Department produces to distribute abroad) equates writing in English to a form of survival, a way "to live a meaningful life."[10] And it makes more sense to hear this not as resistance to literary nationalism but as a success of U.S. cultural diplomacy. In short, no one has told the State Department that a novel influenced by Latin American neorealism is inimical to their cultural diplomacy concerns (and work by Cohn and others has pointed to a more complicated narrative: the CIA was all over this literature during the Cold War). And it might be the opposite.

Just as Casanova notices that "nothing is more international than a national state," so too nothing is more international, or imperial, than empire's nationalist literatures.[11] Any understanding of the geopolitical novel and whether it can meaningfully be a part of new political positions and attitudes and move beyond national forms as Irr claims has to at least address the relationship between U.S. literary production and the state as well as the relationship between the literary production of other nations and the U.S. state. And a complete understanding must also address the atrophied ties that literature has to resistance to imperial globalization. In some ways, when understanding the relationship of this sort of novel and what sorts of nationalism it might manifest one has to consider not just the national origin of its range of reference and allusion but also the language in which it is composed, its distribution networks, and its publication history. The relationship between literature and international organizations like UNESCO, as Brouillette has inventoried, must also be considered. And not just the state, understanding the relationship between literature and all sorts of private institutions that often work in collaboration with the state is also crucial. Irr alludes in her work to how the MFA is one of these forces (even as she dismisses its impact), but the MFA is just one part of this machine.

The Bush administration's response to the accident of history that is 9 / 11 was a moment when this interest that the state has in literature became clearer than usual. Just weeks after September 11, Charlotte Beers, a prominent adwoman often associated with J. Walter Thompson Company, was hired by the U.S. State Department as Undersecretary of State for Public Diplomacy. Thus began what might usefully be seen as an opening volley in a new round of the old fight by the state to occupy literature in English. Among Beers's projects was the publication of an essay collection to be distributed by U.S. embassies called *Writers on America*.[12] The publication could not be distributed within the United States because the Smith-Mundt Act forbade domestic distribution of propaganda materials intended for foreign audiences by the State Department. *Writers on America* features fifteen American writers, among them poets laureate Robert Pinsky and Billy Collins, writing about and celebrating being an American. George Clack, executive editor of the publication, states in his introduction that the publication "could illuminate in an interesting way certain America[n] values—freedom, diversity, democracy—that may not be well understood in all parts of the world.[13] With obvious nationalism, the writers featured in *Writers on America* promote U.S. freedoms. Much of the work omits the negative role that the U.S. government plays in the lives of many of its citizens and does not reference the hugely detrimental impact that the U.S. government has had on the lives of citizens of other nations. The publication is, of course, fairly multicultural and features many writers whose work is concerned with immigration (Elmaz Abinader, Julia Alvarez, Bharati Mukherjee, and Naomi Shihab Nye) as well as Native writers (Linda Hogan) writing about the advantages they have received from being included within the U.S. nation building project. Nye, for instance, writes "Everything was possible in the United States—this was not just a rumor, it was *true*. He [her father] might not grow rich overnight, but he could sell insurance, import colorful gifts from around the world, start little stores, become a journalist. He could do *anything*."[14]

But it is not just that the Bush administration amps up the classic moves of mid-century cultural diplomacy. It also is attentive to the role that literature plays within the United States. Prior to Bush and prior to September 11, the National Endowment for the Arts was much besieged. Basically, each year that Clinton was in office the National Endowment for the Arts budget was cut. When he was inaugurated in 1993, its budget was $174 million. When he left office in 2001, it was $104 million. Despite the Bush administration's rhetoric of small government and of cutting subsidies to a liberal elite, each year he was in office the National Endowment for the Arts' budget went up. By 2009, $57 million of the $69 million cut from the National Endowment for the Arts under Clinton had been returned.[15] (And 2010's appropriation of over $167 million would be as high as the budget would go; it decreased each year Obama was in office; increases or decreases interestingly correlate more to the party of the presidency than to which party controls Congress.) To oversee this largess, the administration appointed Dana Gioia, a former vice president at General Foods and one of many businessman-poets associated with the Bush administration, as chairman in 2003. Gioia immediately declared his agenda to take "the agency beyond the culture wars."[16] And this desire can be seen in the fairly mundane series of initiatives that he established during his tenure: Shakespeare in American Communities (a program that funds professional Shakespeare troupes to perform in schools), the Big Read (a program that funds various communities to read a book out of a list of twenty-six approved books, all of them realist novels or short stories with the exception of selections of poems by Emily Dickinson and Robinson Jeffers), Jazz Masters (support for jazz performances), Poetry Out Loud (a poetry recitation contest for high school students), and Operation Homecoming (a series of writing workshops and publications for troops and their spouses).

Of all of these fairly tepid projects, Operation Homecoming is the most obvious example of the militarized dimensions of literary nationalism. Operation Homecoming created fifty writing workshops that were attended by 6,000 troops and their spouses and published the anthology *Operation Homecoming: Iraq, Afghanistan, and the Home Front, in the Words of U.S. Troops and Their Families*. Operation Homecoming was also a partnership between the National Endowment for the Arts, the Poetry Foundation, and Boeing, so it hit all sectors of the creative economy (the state, private foundations, and private companies). And while this sort of programming was not treated as a secret in the CIA sort of way, it is not a big part of the Poetry Foundation's public face. For instance, *Poetry* (the "little" magazine that is the Poetry Foundation's reason for being) published a critique of the project by Eleanor Wilner and did not mention that the foundation was funding this project at the same time.[17] Gioia wrote the preface to *Operation Homecoming: Iraq, Afghanistan, and the Home Front, in the Words of U.S. Troops and Their Families*. It is full of anxiety; he states at least three times that the book is not an "official" government publication: "It is not an official publication"; "The Department of Defense played no role in selecting the contents of the book"; "Someone suggested the book be marketed as the first 'official' account of the war, but 'official' is exactly what *Operation Homecoming* is not."[18] He also claims that "there is something in *Operation Homecoming* to support every viewpoint on the war—whatever the political stance."[19] But he is, as one might imagine, exaggerating. While there is some talk about the horrors of war, there is little analysis that connects the recent wars to U.S. imperialism, an analysis that one might expect from an anthology promising to represent every viewpoint on the war.

Steve Evans in "Free (Market) Verse" also notices the peculiar interest that the Bush administration had in literature and he charts it through the rise of a group of poets that he calls "Poets for Bush." "Through men like Dana Gioia, John Barr, and Ted Kooser," Evans writes, "Karl Rove's battle-tested blend of unapologetic economic elitism and reactionary cultural populism is now being marketed in the far-off reaches of the poetry world."[20] Evans begins his article with Ruth Lilly's endowment of nearly $200 million that resulted in the establishment of the Poetry Foundation in 2003 (the magazine received the original Lilly bequest and the foundation was established to manage the bequest) with Barr as the president, a position he held until 2013. When he was appointed president, he was a minor poet at best and better known as a banker. His banking career began at Morgan Stanley, where Barr specialized in utility mergers. During this time, he also was founder and chairman of the Natural Gas Clearing-house, now known as Dynegy. He left Morgan Stanley and, in 1990, cofounded the boutique firm Barr Devlin. Barr Devlin oversaw some 40 percent of the dollar volume on utilities mergers between 1990 and 1996.[21] In 1998, Société Générale bought Barr Devlin, giving the firm international reach and support. That same year, the Power Company of America, LP, a firm largely owned by the same people who owned Barr Devlin, was one of the first power trading companies to default, serving as an early warning of the vulnerability of a deregulated market.[22] Shortly thereafter Dynegy, like Enron, was accused of price manipulation and other fraudulent practices during the California electricity crisis. And in the way that literature, the state, private founda-tions, and higher education all worked together in the United States at the turn of the twenty-first century, Barr's career em-bodies all of these. He was also chairman of the board at Ben-nington College when it abolished tenure and fired a third of its faculty in 1994, giving it the distinction of being at the forefront of what is now the long march toward an increasingly casualized faculty in the academy.[23]

Lilly's endowment instantly put the Poetry Foundation in the front lines of U.S. arts organizations. (Just for comparison, the net assets of the Poetry Project tend to be a little less than a mil-lion and a half and for Cave Canem somewhere between $300,000 and a half million.) Evans ends with a list of the changes that he says "rhymed with the Poetry bequest."[24] These include "the aes-thetically conservative poetry insider" Ed Hirsch being picked to preside over the John Simon Guggenheim Foundation in 2002 and the 2003 appointment of Gioia as the National Endowment for the Arts chairman.[25] Although he tends to present as a democrat, I might add Garrison Keillor to Evans's list. Keillor distributes his folksy defenses of white ethnicity in his various government funded productions such as National Public Radio's *A Prairie Home Companion, The Writer's Almanac,* and the Public Broadcasting Service's short film series Poetry Everywhere. And Keillor, Barr, and Gioia often worked together during the Bush years. Barr lists in his 2006 "annual report to the poetry community" that the Poetry Foundation is "a major sponsor" of *The Writer's Almanac.*[26] Keillor has returned a favor as a judge for the National Endowment for the Arts / Poetry Foundation's Poetry Out Loud. And Keillor's various projects provide an interesting example of how these writers often overlap in print publications. Barr, Gioia, and Kooser have all had poems (sometimes numerous poems) featured in *The Writer's Almanac*; Gioia and Kooser have also been prominently included in many of Keillor's *Good Poems* anthologies (a print spin-off of his National Public Radio programs). Barr was on the editorial panel of *Operation Homecoming.*

Evans concentrates not just on the usual cronyism that defines contemporary literary production, but he also makes an aesthetic argument. His noticing here has a certain truth: the poets that the Poets for Bush promoted and supported with their funds tended to fit Casanova's claim that a nationalist poet reproduces in the language of the nation not only the "most conventional but also the most consistent with commercial—which is to say national, universally outmoded—criteria."[27] The work that the Poets for Bush put their money behind was usually written in English and was of mundane subject matter. Kooser is an interesting example here. As its president, Barr put the Poetry Foundation's monetary muscle behind Kooser and it often feels as if Kooser sprang out of obscurity because of a combination of the poet laureate position (he, like Collins, held the position twice under Bush) and the Poetry Foundation. It is not as if Kooser had done nothing before 2004, the year he was awarded the poet laureate position, the first year of the Poetry Foundation's operations, and the year that Kooser's *Delights and Shadows* was published. At the time, he was in his mid-sixties and had published a number of books with undistinguished presses to minimal critical attention. Gioia, one of few people to write about Kooser prior to 2004, argues in "The Anonymity of the Regional Poet" that Kooser was invisible because he was a regional poet and, as a result, the system was stacked against him: "His fellow poets look on him as an anomaly or an anachronism. Reviewers find him eminently unnewsworthy. Publishers see little prestige attached to printing his work. Critics, who have been trained to celebrate complexity, consider him an amiable simpleton."[28] It is underestimating Kooser to see him as an amiable simpleton, but there is no denying that this is the persona that he presents not just in his overall-wearing, Adirondack-chair-sitting author photographs but also in his work. Kooser's Pulitzer Prize–winning *Delights and Shadows,* for instance, begins with a poem about walking on tiptoe, a poem about a faded tattoo, a poem about a woman with cancer walking into a cancer clinic, and a poem about a student walking into a library.

For its part, the Poetry Foundation invested a lot in proving that Kooser's "unnewsworthiness" was no longer true. One of the foundation's inaugural programs was the founding of "American Life in Poetry," a website that featured a "brief" and "enjoyable" poem by a poet and an even shorter commentary about the poem by Kooser. The program's mission, for reasons that remain unclear, was to get poetry into midsized and rural newspapers. In a 2005 press release, the Poetry Foundation claims that over seventy newspapers ran the column.[29] These brief and enjoyable poems are, Casanova might argue, English-only, conventional, and outmoded. Standard English not only defines Kooser's newspaper poems project, but also his patriotically titled *Writing Brave and Free* (written with Steve Cox), a book of writing advice for those new to writing that states, "Writing doesn't use another language, but the language we're already using."[30] The statement feels as if it could be as mundane as the poem about walking on tiptoe except behind its purported populist advice is a dismissal not only of one of the ways writers at least attempt to be autonomous from literary nationalism but also of how languages other than English might be a constitutive part of the lives of many U.S. citizens.

Keillor's *Good Poems* anthologies are also full of this sort of brief and enjoyable (Standard English only, conventional, and outmoded) poem. And again, one could just notice the attention to the everyday, to the mundane moment in these poems as idiosyncratic if a rhetoric of populism was not being used to cover a sort of nationalist cronyism perpetuated by businessmen poets. There is no clearer example of this cronyism than Gioia's review of Keillor's *Good Poems* anthology that was published in *Poetry*. *Good Poems* includes a poem by Gioia—"Summer Storm"—which would disqualify him from being a reviewer at most publications. But this conflict of interest does not stop Gioia from repeatedly setting Keillor's anthology against an imagined elitism that would dismiss it. The anthology "épater la bourgeoisie, at least academic bourgeoisie," he claims; "The politesse and meekness of Po-Biz insiders is blissfully absent from his lively assessments of American poets"; "not a volume aimed at academic pursuits but at ordinary human purposes"; it "restores faith in the possibilities of public culture."[31] The claim of faith in public culture is particularly dissimilating. It requires putting aside the lack of economic analysis that lets Gioia present Keillor and himself as saving poetry from the bourgeoisie. It is not just Barr and Gioia that have business backgrounds: Kooser is a former vice president of Lincoln Benefit Life Company and Keillor's net worth from the *Prairie Home Companion* and its spin-offs is significant. And it requires not noticing that this is for an anthology that, as Rita Dove points out in a letter to the editor of *Poetry,* has 294 poems, yet includes "only three Black poets—all of them dead, no less, and the one woman actually a blues singer."[32] Dove's analysis, of course, is only the start of any accounting one might do of who is included in the definition of "public" here.

While I do not want to make too much out of these conventional and outmoded works, to ignore them risks ignoring a fairly significant form of U.S. poetry production at the turn of the century. And it also risks underestimating the relentless way that a bunch of businessmen poets claim a certain control over literature and exert this control not only through government and foundation alliances, not only through budgets in the hundreds of millions, but also through a series of intellectually suspect assertions. Again and again a sort of counter-insurgent rhetoric is used by the Poets for Bush to attack autonomous aesthetics. In "American Poetry in the New Century" Barr counterintuitively claims that "modernism has passed into the DNA of the MFA programs."[33] Modernism in Barr's mind is corrupting: "For all its schools and experiments, contemporary poetry is still written in the rain shadow thrown by Modernism. It is the engine that drives what is written today. And it is a tired engine."[34] Gioia in "Can Poetry Matter?" admits that "occasionally a writer links up rewardingly to a social or political movement," but then he continues, "It is a difficult task to marry the Muse happily to politics. Consequently, most contemporary poets, knowing they are virtually invisible in the larger culture, focus on the more intimate forms of lyric and meditative verse."[35] Joseph Epstein in his essay "Who Killed Poetry?" also worries similarly. He answers his own question with higher education, grants, and poets who "parade as spokesmen and -women for their ethnic group or race or political tendency."[36]

But once again political concerns are not aesthetically rigid or limited to the most conventional of aesthetics. There is no better example of the diversity of aesthetic tactics that these businessmen use in their attack on an autonomous, linguistically independent literature than Barr's epic poem *Grace,* published in 1999 by Story Line Press. While *Grace* is not a major work in turn of the century literature, I have long thought of it as telling. Barr writes *Grace* in another English, in what the ancillary materials to the book call "a Caribbean-like speech."[37] But its intention seems to be to attack the idea that work not written in Standard English is autonomous. It is telling that Barr decides to use not only blackface but also an aestheticized dialect as the language of composition, a form that is more or less, despite its early associations with minstrel traditions, mainly used in the last half of the twentieth century by writers as a signifier for inclusive linguistic rights, for imperial critique. *Grace* fits the understanding of dialect literature by scholars such as Michael North, where dialect is a form in which racial divisions are upheld and imagined ethnic threats are countered. This formula is, of course, not universally true. Gavin Jones's *Strange Talk* spent some time on exceptions to this in the nineteenth century. And in the twentieth, one might point to works by Claude McKay. But it does well describe *Grace* and it is hard to read *Grace* with anything but open-mouthed wonder. Barr's *Grace* is a bold defense of empire, one that indulges in blackface in order to do so for Barr willingly admits to corking his face when he states in an interview that *Grace* was his "opportunity to take a fresh look at everything I wanted to talk about when I was approaching the age of 50."[38]

Grace tells the story of Ibn Opcit, a character who well exemplifies the happy-go-lucky darky stereotype of the minstrel tradition. Ibn Opcit is a gardener of the Overruth estate who is condemned to die by the court system of what is called the "Carib Kingdom." His crime was witnessing the husband of "ballbuster of de first magnitude" Mistress Hepatica Overruth kill her lover Flavian Wyoming after he walks in on them having anal sex.[39] Or that is how I am reading the phrase "den he settle his equipment in de lady's outback."[40] The language here is loaded and bawdy, sexualized and racialized. Barr writes of Wyoming and Overruth, "De gentlemen, he produce his produce / like a corporate salami, and she hers, / like a surgery scar still angry red wid healing."[41] At another moment, when Ibn Opcit describes how he was watering the plants when he saw the murder, the judge asks "was de hose / you holdin' in your hand a garden hose / or was it your black natural own?"[42] *Grace,* in other words is uniquely racist and sexist, often at the same time.

This happens in the first six pages of the book. The rest of the book seems to be Ibn Opcit's prison ramblings to someone named Geode. The six chapters that follow have Ibn Opcit talking mainly about America and how great it is. Although there is undeniably a parodic element to Ibn Opcit's proclamations, Barr rarely has him say anything in critique, parodic or otherwise about the empire that is America. The America that he describes is unfaltering. It has "an economy that hums / like a hamper of flies, where the top line and the bottom / are in easy walking distance."[43] In the first chapter, Ibn Opcit briefly sketches a series of male figures that represent America: Eddy Ubbjer (a businessman of some sort), Engarde Monocutter (a poet), Spillman Sponneker (a politician), and Contemptible Bede (a pastor). Barr follows this with a brief chapter of "The Opposite Number" in which Ibn Opcit shares his thoughts on women. In this Carib Kingdom, women do not seem to have professions. And Ibn Opcit's observations rarely go deeper than observations that wives lose interest in sex: "you happen like thunder over her; / she happen like earthquake under you / . . . Pretty soon, though, she prone to a natural disinterest."[44] If this "natural disinterest" does not happen, apparently they become whorish and likely to grab their riding teacher's "Walcott." One of the peculiarities of this book is how Barr racializes sexual terms; he not only uses the name of Derek Walcott as a euphemism for the penis but he also calls an orgasm a "Sakajaweha." All of this ends with Ibn Opcit asking the profound questions of "How many men marry an ass? / How many women, a portfolio?"[45] In the chapters that follow, more stories of various male figures are told. The poem concludes with Ibn Opcit perhaps escaping from jail; it is unclear if it should be read as fantasy or as actual.

Adding irony to that claim about wanting to take poetry back from modernism, in an interview with Michael Useem Barr says "poets should be imperialists."[46] And he continues, "I think they should be importers; I think they should be exploiters of external experience, without apology."[47] The way that he does so in *Grace* is by demeaning and mocking modernism and its attention to what Jolas often called the revolution of the word. Ibn Opcit like many blackface characters not only is in awe of empire but he demeans all things not of empire. Not only does he demean his own national literary traditions with the Walcott-penis joke, he also manages to demean through sexual euphemism those with similar histories of colonization, such as Native Americans of the continental United States and the Pacific, with lines like "Perhaps he tickle her in de snickly abode / until she Sakajaweha. Maybe she hold him / by de long-neck until he Eniwetok."[48] One has to wonder what region Rick Moody has in mind when he suggests in his blurb that *Grace* is "attempting sympathy" and is "crucial for the regional literature."[49]

Part of me wants to apologize for spending so much time on *Grace*. It is not as if the book has been prized or well-received. And the literary scholar part of me that looks for excellent and meaningful literature feels a bit stupid taking it so seriously. Other than a four-paragraph blog post by Kent Johnson and a mention of it in Dana Goodyear's article in the *New Yorker* on the Poetry Foundation, there is almost no discussion of this book, scholarly or otherwise.[50] Contemporary literary scholarship tends to present literature as a resistant project, as an antiracist one. Even critiques of how race is represented in U.S. literature tend not to be focused on literature that is clearly and obviously racist. If one just read post-45 scholarship and looked at post-45 anthologies, one would believe that contemporary literature is both very racially inclusive and more or less antiracist in content. I have only read *Grace,* I admit, because I am interested in Barr's role as president of the Poetry Foundation. But at the same time, it is not merely that Barr plays a large role in setting the tone and direction of contemporary literature production at the turn of the century. *Grace* does have two editions. Story Line Press published *Grace* on its own in 1999. And then in 2013, Red Hen Press thought it was important enough to bring it back into print in a hardback boxed set with a sequel: *Opcit at Large*.[51] While these publications could be more indicative of Barr's institutional power than of a readership, *Grace* is still a part of contemporary U.S. literature. And understandings of how contemporary U.S. literature functions should at least be able to recognize and reckon with it.

As much as it would have made this book easier to write to have ignored *Grace* (and by the standards of literary scholarship, this would not necessarily have been seen as negligence), I do not think one can understand the forces that will come to define literary production at the turn of the twenty-first century without taking Barr's provocations in *Grace* seriously. If there is anything to be learned from *Grace* it is that there is something complicated here in this relationship between language and the state. *Grace* is just interesting because it is unusually explicit in its racism. And while *Grace* is something of an outlier formally, its politics will be made manifest in all sorts of other ways at the turn of twenty-first century.

The plain speech folksy poems that Evans calls "Poets for Bush" (and also Barr's very much related attack on a poetry of linguistic autonomy) was just one form among many that literary nationalism took at the turn of the century. Although I am not that interested in poetry's various electoral party affiliations, this sort of poetry has tended to skew more Republican than not. Another is the inaugural poem, a form of poetry that has only been used by the Democratic party. It is probably not a coincidence that the very small genre of the inaugural poem (there are only five examples) cluster at the turn of the century. Prior to Clinton's inauguration, there is only one example within the American literary canon and it is a complicated one: Robert Frost's reading for John F. Kennedy's 1961 inauguration. Frost wrote "Dedication" for this event, but the glare and the wind made it impossible for him to read it so instead he recited from memory his nationalist

"The Gift Outright," a poem that begins "The land was ours before we were the land's."[52] If ever there has been a nationalist poet,
it has been Frost. He willingly embraces the position, writing in
a letter to Régis Michaud, "the national is the root of all thought
and art."[53] "The Gift Outright" was a major poem for Frost. As
Jeff Westover notes, "When Frost recited the poem from memory
at the inauguration, he delivered a text that had been rendered
public many times, in the published form of his various selected
and collected poems (1946, 1949, 1954, 1955) and in the oral form
of his many public readings."[54] It also is a stunning example poem
of that stubborn relationship between poetry and nationalism
that Eliot noticed. "The Gift Outright" is a poem of five sentences
divided into sixteen lines. The first three state that the "land" (the
United States) belongs to the immigrants, each one worrying this
owning with a similar phrase: "The land was ours . . ."; "She was
our land . . ."; "She was ours . . ."[55] The immigrants, the poem
makes clear, belonged to England. The poem is almost a sonnet,
it turns with the fifth sentence (the eighth line): the immigrants
realize they have been withholding themselves from the land and
then in the last sentence, which provides a sonnet's couplet-esque
summary, give themselves to the land and give a gift of many
wars. My description risks making a highly crafted poem sound
more trite than it is. By all the standards of official verse, this
poem is solidly made. It is also resonant without being cloying. I
respect its craft. But it also is a poem that is shocking in its blind-
ness to the genocide of the native peoples and its naturalization
of the colonization of the United States.

And it is just as telling that there are no more inaugural poems
for the next twenty-five or so years, for after 1965 poetry in particular became a genre with a thriving relationship with resistance in the United States. And it is just as telling that it is

Clinton who brought the inaugural poem back when he had Maya Angelou perform "On the Pulse of Morning" at his 1993 inauguration, for by 1993 poetry had switched back to become a genre more associated with accommodation than with resistance. How this happened is the story I am telling in this book. But outside of that story, there are some obvious other reasons why Clinton would have an inaugural poet. Among the many PR moves made by Clinton's campaign was one that compared him to Kennedy and his administration's move to commission a poem for his 1993 inauguration was frequently seen as an allusion to Kennedy. And the decision that it be Angelou is perhaps another way of reinforcing the often circulated idea that he was, as Toni Morrison claimed in the *New Yorker* in 1998, the nation's "first black president."[56] Angelou is also a poet with a long history of working for the state. She began her career as an actor in the State Department's twenty-two nation tour of *Porgy and Bess.*

The story that is told about the odd genre of the inaugural poem is inconsistent (all the forces that I am attempting to trace here develop unevenly). The poem that Miller Williams wrote, "Of History and Hope," for Clinton's 1997 (second) inauguration is probably the most conventional in its nationalism, the poem most in the tradition of Frost. It is in Standard English and it is more or less lyric nationalism. Williams opens his poem with "We have memorized America, / how it was born and who we have been and where" and, as if he has also memorized Anderson's *Imagined Communities,* he literally imagines the imagined community of U.S. citizen into existence: "Who were many people coming together / cannot become one people falling apart."[57] Its nationalism is so legible and traditional that it would be absurd to spend time on the poem.

I am, however, more interested in Angelou's "On the Pulse of Morning" because it provides such a clear example of how the state at the turn of the century recuperated a certain form of multiculturalism for its nationalist concerns. The poem begins with dinosaurs, but it then turns to do the work that a state poem does: encourage the many people who reside in the United States to imagine themselves as part of one national citizenship. So it echoes Williams's sentiment of one people coming together under a national subjectivity, but it abandons the more refined and unified lyric tonality and subjectivity that he uses (the Frost tradition). Instead it uses the cataloguing list of separate identity categories that is such a crucial part of multicultural poetry:

> So say the Asian, the Hispanic, the Jew
> The African, the Native American, the Sioux,
> The Catholic, the Muslim, the French, the Greek
> The Irish, the Rabbi, the Priest, the Sheik,
> The Gay, the Straight, the Preacher,
> The privileged, the homeless, the Teacher.[58]

And then two stanzas later, the nation speaks:

> You, who gave me my first name, you
> Pawnee, Apache, Seneca, you
> Cherokee Nation, . . .
> You, the Turk, the Arab, the Swede, the German, the Eskimo,
>   the Scot,
> You the Ashanti, the Yoruba, the Kru,[59]

Angelou's poem is formally similar to something like Gonzales's *I Am Joaquin,* but it lacks the analysis of the economic conditions of racism and the cultural separatism and the calls for resistance to white supremacy. In this it clearly demonstrates how the state moves in to recuperate resistant forms and then empties them of their content as it brings them into literary nationalism. As C. O. Grossman writes, "the rhetorical thrust of these poems is . . . a vision of social and cultural unification under the banner of national citizenship."[60] The nationalism of Frost's poem argues that an "American" is a European immigrant. Angelou's poem written to support the state's multicultural politics of acknowledgment adds Native Americans, other sorts of immigrants, and also those forcibly brought to the United States through slavery and unites them, asking them to recognize "their" country without critique as it invokes them to "look up and out / and into your sister's eyes, and into / Your brother's face, your country, And say simply / Very simply / With hope— / Good morning."[61]

The other two existing inaugural poems essentially do the same thing. Elizabeth Alexander's "Praise Song for the Day," written for Obama's 2009 inauguration, also has the listing of possible national subjectivities even if hers are more a listing by profession: a farmer, a teacher, the many who "have died for this day" "who laid the train tracks, raised the bridges, / / picked the cotton and the lettuce, built / brick by brick the glittering edifices / they would then keep clean and work inside of."[62] And Richard Blanco's "One Today" abandons the deliberate listing of identity categories and replaces it (and Angelou's good morning) with the word "hello" in immigrant languages other than English:

the doors we open
for each other all day, saying: hello, shalom,
buon giorno, howdy, namaste, or buenos días

in the language my mother taught me—in every language
spoken into one wind carrying our lives
without prejudice, as these words break from my lips.[63]

The emphasis in Blanco's poem is on geographic boundaries. This
is one way his poem shows the obligatory debt to Frost. Also similar to Frost, an American identity is an immigrant identity in
this poem. And when Blanco claims to be "the first openly gay,
first immigrant, and first Latino inaugural poet" in *For All of Us,
One Today: An Inaugural Poet's Journey* he is right about being
the first openly gay and Latino inaugural poet.[64] But all of the inaugural poets might be considered to be immigrants as none
identify as Native American (even as he might by immigrant be
talking about how he was born in Spain and moved to the United
States when he was less than two months old). It also is perhaps
the most nationalist of all these poems. It opens with the lines
"One sun rose on us today, kindled over our shores, / peeking over
the Smokies, greeting the faces / of the Great Lakes, spreading a
simple truth / across the Great Plains, then charging across the
Rockies."[65] Harris Feinsod calls this sun "an overdetermined
symbol of national unification, rising and setting on a singular
nation, illuminating a movement of westward expansion (from
the Smokies to the Great Lakes and the Great Plains to the
Rockies)," a "revival of the rhetorical drift of manifest destiny."[66]
Blanco then returns to this theme towards the end: "One sky:
since the Appalachians and Sierras claimed / their majesty, and
the Mississippi and Colorado worked / their way to the sea."[67] It
is a poem built around the idea of there being one country: "One
ground. Our ground."[68]

The inaugural poems are odd and specific examples. And I
confess that I have brought them into this discussion so they

might function as a sort of strawpoem. For it is when putting something like Blanco's imagining of "one sun, "one sky," and "One ground. Our ground" next to Kim's assertion to "translate: 38th parallel" that it becomes obvious that these poems have very different relations to nationalism. Blanco's poem has clear national boundaries that, say, Gómez-Peña's or Kim's work repeatedly break down.

None of these moments are isolated examples. The commingling of literary and state and military concerns that defined Operation Homecoming is fairly common. The Poetry Foundation also partnered with the National Endowment for the Arts and Boeing on the Big Read, a program that encouraged communities, including military bases, to read and discuss works of literature. The National Endowment for the Arts has partnered with the Department of Defense in a creative arts therapy program. The National Endowment for the Humanities has partnered with various not for profits in programs such as the Warrior Scholar Project, Dialogues on the Experience of War, and Books on Bases. These overlaps are also particularly clear with PEN America, even as there is no evidence that PEN is as close to the CIA as it was in the middle of the twentieth century. However, it still maintains a symbiotic relationship with national security interests. A recent PEN conference on "The Future of Truth" featured a panel that included General Michael Hayden (retired Air Force General, former director of the Central Intelligence Agency and National Security Agency), Susan Hennessey (former attorney, Office of General Counsel of the National Security Agency, Brookings Institution Fellow in National Security in Governance Studies), David Sanger (chief Washington correspondent, the *New York Times*), and Vikram Singh (vice president of national security and international policy, Center for American Progress, former deputy assistant secretary of defense for South and South-east Asia at the Pentagon, senior advisor on Afghanistan and Pakistan for the Department of Defense; Singh also ran a Ford Foundation program on minority rights in Bangladesh, India, Nepal, Pakistan, and Sri Lanka). Further, as in the 1950s, the socialities of private foundations and the government are inter-twined. Ford Foundation president Darren Walker is a member of the Council on Foreign Relations. Henry Bienen, current pres-ident of the Poetry Foundation, has served as a consultant to the State Department, the National Security Council, the Agency for International Development, the CIA, the World Bank, and Boeing. Suzanne Nossel, executive director of PEN America, brags about working at her previous role as deputy assistant sec-retary of state for international organizations at the U.S. Depart-ment of State in her bio. This list is just the beginning of overlaps.

As it has since the middle of the century, and no matter the party affiliation of the president, the State Department and its various agencies continue to send writers abroad for reasons of cultural diplomacy. The aesthetics of U.S. cultural diplomacy tend to be more aligned with the Clinton and Obama (and the private foundations of the late 1960s / early 1970s) aesthetics than with the Poets for Bush. The diplomatic cables from 2003–2010 that were released by Wikileaks document how the State Department uses multicultural writers for their cultural diplomacy: "Na-tasha Tretheway enlightened young Omani audiences about the compelling history of African-Americans and their contribu-tion to broader American society and engendered lively discus-sion between the speakers and their audiences"; Gina Loring did a program where "each of the students was encouraged to write about social issues in Kuwait and to be candid about areas for improvement in governance, and then put it all together in a single play"; "Many of the students were moved by Ms. Moss' poignant life story and the profundity of her poetry and philosophy. At one point the Skype connection lost sound but a local translator volunteered to read a poem by African-American poet Marilyn Henson, who had visited Yekaterinburg the year before."[69] The cables are, as always, optimistic about the impact of cultural diplomacy: "The program reinforced American values, included valuing diversity, the underlying theme of Black History Month," a March 19, 2009, cable claims about an Ilene Evans presentation.[70] About a Loring presentation in Kuwait, an April 18, 2007, cable notes: "The Gina Loring group's visit coincided with the Embassy's celebration of African American History Month and provided an ideal opportunity to teach Kuwaiti youth about the value of diversity within American society. . . . By underscoring African American cultural contributions to American society through music, and reaching sizeable and unique new audiences, this program far exceeded the expectations of the original Performing Arts Initiative proposal. . . . Despite questions regarding the appropriateness of this type of music for Kuwait audiences raised prior to implementation of the program, the group proved exceptional at achieving audience participation and winning over conservative audiences."[71] The local press in various locations at moments though tells a different story. The newspaper *Millyet* bemusedly reported that a Loring performance in Turkey in 2011 had an audience of twenty people who wandered by.[72]

However, it is important to note that it is not just multicultural or plain speech literature that interested the state during this time. At the turn of the twenty-first century, more and more often, poets associated with what Casanova would consider autonomous literature were reading for "Reading Abroad: American Writers on Tour," a series of State Department–funded literary tours to places in the Middle East and Africa, or were serving on the board of the International Writing Program. In recent years, Eleni Sikelianos presented work in Cambodia and Vietnam; Annie Finch and Laird Hunt in the Congo; Bob Holman and Ram Devineni in Nepal, Afghanistan, United Arab Emirates, and Pakistan; Major Jackson and Eliot Weinberger in Kenya; Katie Ford and Weinberger in Tunis; Olena Kalytiak Davis in the Middle East; Joyelle McSweeney, Matt Hart, Amanda Nadelberg, Shin Yu Pai in China; Terrance Hayes and Matthew Zapruder in Russia; Alison Deming and Cornelius Eady in Brazil.[73] Ilya Kaminsky, Charles Simic, Cole Swenson, and Weinberger are all on the advisory board for the International Writing Program.[74] But not just reading abroad, also reading at the White House. In 2011, Kenneth Goldsmith performed at the Obama White House at an event that included Elizabeth Alexander, Billy Collins, Common, Rita Dove, Alison Knowles, Aimee Mann, Jill Scott, and Steve Martin and the Steep Canyon Rangers.

Two things interest me here. One is that something new is happening: literature that might possibly be categorized as autonomous because of its avant garde ties is American enough and safe enough to be incorporated not just into cultural diplomacy (the history of cultural diplomacy has traditionally not worried about aesthetics much) but into U.S. nationalism. The White House in 2011 did not see Goldsmith (or Knowles, also long involved in experimental traditions) as being a meaningful part of resistance to the state, did not see their avant garde aesthetics as unfit or as contesting literary nationalism. But even more interesting is that writers are willing participants. The decision to read, and to accept rewards given by, the White House has been one that is often vexed for writers and artists, and poets in particular have a long tradition of refusing (there is often, as Casanova's work suggests, more to be gained from appearing autonomous than from accepting state accolades). Adrienne Rich refused the National Medal for the Arts in 1997, under the Clinton administration.[75] And in 2003, Laura Bush attempted to set up an event honoring Hughes, Dickinson, and Whitman that was eventually canceled after several of the poets she had invited made their distaste with the various wars of the Bush administration clear and declared their intentions to further clarify this at the event or refused to attend. Dove was among these poets. And so was Sam Hamill, who in addition to declining also encouraged poets to send antiwar poems to Laura Bush. He then set up the popular Poets Against the War website and invited individuals to submit "a poem or statement of conscience."[76] Over 13,000 poets had submitted before the site stopped accepting new poems. But the idea that poetry should be in the most minor of ways resistance to U.S. wars was gone by 2011. It was so gone that when Vanessa Place published a defense of Goldsmith's reading at the White House on the Poetry Foundation blog—she complained about the "equally empty argument that it is the duty of the avant garde not to 'play minstrel' for the Man"—it is completely unclear who has made this empty argument about Goldsmith.[77] (It's an odd piece in other ways also. It is both celebratory of the "historically parodic and complex role" of the minstrel tradition and also intensely dismissive of Common and Dove; Place calls Dove's wisdom "odoriferous.")[78] And it remains gone. In 2017, Major Jackson edited a "Renga for Obama" for the *Harvard Review*. It featured over 200 poets celebrating "the exemplary way in which he has carried out his duty," which "represents the very best of who we are—a nation bonded by a high regard for freedom and the arts as a carrier of our most treasured values."[79]

There is no better example of the strength of that stubborn relationship.

There are many reasons that writers and performers use to justify reading at the White House or writing a poem celebrating a president. There are, of course, those who eagerly work this circuit, some of them justifying reading at the White House with a but-my-writing-is-so-important-that-it-might-perhaps-change-the-course-of-empire sort of argument, some of them just unrepentant nationalists. Parts of this story are probably about how some writers and performers can be as serenely passive in the face of state brutality as politicians. Parts of it could be about how some might be fine with state brutality when its party affiliation is Democrat. Dove's behavior seems to suggest the latter. Aside from declining to read at the Laura Bush event, she has been a willing nationalist poet. She has served two terms as the poet laureate. She has received both the National Humanities Medal and the National Medal of Arts. She read at the 1996 Olympics. She read for Clinton at the White House. And she is married to Fred Viebahn, who, as her bio explains, came to the United States as a participant in the State Department's International Writing Program.

Higher education is often seen as independent of government and private foundations. But as Stefano Harney and Fred Moten point out in *The Undercommons,* "the Universitas is always a state/State strategy."[80] And higher education has also played a significant, and in many cases very similar, role in amplifying the institutionalization of literature and it intensifies in interesting ways at the turn of the twenty-first century. What McGurl notices about the closeness between higher education and U.S. literary production at mid-century is even more true at the turn of the century, even as the connections that Bennett charts in mid-century developments of the MFA will play less of a role in shaping the discipline (the discipline had been shaped so there was no need to continue this sort of funding). The economic pressures that define higher education at the end of the century are not incentive funding from foundations and the State Department but the opposite: dwindling resources have forced higher education to be more market-driven. Prior to the 1990s and the intensifying financial pressures that brought about the corporatization of the university, English departments tended to have a studious lack of interest that bordered on disdain about the teaching of creative writing. (And top-tier schools still tend to not offer graduate degrees in creative writing. Of the top ten universities, according to *USNWR* rankings, only Columbia has an MFA program.[81]) But in 1992, Higher Education Amendments increased student loan limits and added the possibility of unsubsidized loans, thereby dramatically expanding the number of students eligible to borrow. The Higher Education Amendments allowed colleges and universities to raise tuition at staggering rates over the last twenty years and at the same time to expand the pool of potential consumers. The result is a large increase in the number of degrees awarded in the field of creative writing in the United States. In 1995 (this is the first year that IPEDS begins reporting creative writing degrees as a separate category from English), fewer than 2,000 people were awarded MFAs in the United States each year. This number steadily increased so that by 2016, close to 5,000 are awarded annually. Basically from 2000 to 2016, around 60,000 people paid money (or paid in labor as teaching assistants) to get a credential that said they have been trained in how to write literature.[82] And it is not just that preexisting programs are graduating more students. There is also a massive increase in the number of programs that offer the degree. In 1984, a little more than 300 programs offered some sort of degree in creative writing (from an associates to a PhD); in 2014 that number had grown to over 1,700.[83] This was an increase of 442 percent; master's programs in creative writing increased by 639 percent.

McGurl ends *The Program Era* with an optimistic diagnosis about higher education's role in twentieth-century literary production. In McGurl's telling higher education is egalitarian and easily accessible. He concludes *The Program Era* with a series of rhetorical questions: "Do we not bear daily witness to a surfeit of literary excellence, an embarrassment of riches? Is there not more excellent fiction being produced now than anyone has time to read? What kind of traitor to the mission of mass higher education would you have to be to think otherwise?"[84] But there are many reasons to be at least a little hesitant to view this as an embarrassment of riches. It takes some dissimulation, for instance, to look at higher education and think its mission is one of mass education. Most obviously, it is a provisionally permeable pay to play community that is constituted through a series of limitations such as applications that the community who enters into it does not control and does not have the right to contest (aka privatized). And while an increasing number of U.S. citizens earn a degree of some sort, this does not necessarily indicate a level playing field. Higher education is a rigorously hierarchical, prestige based system that is almost impossible to talk about in the aggregate because of the huge structural differences between something like University of Phoenix and Yale. Further, as "The Equality of Opportunity Project" points out: "Access to colleges varies substantially across the income distribution. At Ivy League colleges such as Columbia University . . . more students come from families in the top 1% of the income distribution than the bottom half of the income distribution."[85] Also education is becoming less and less accessible to low-income students. They continue: "The fraction

of students from low-income families at the Ivy-Plus colleges increased very little over the period 2000–2011" and "access at institutions with the highest mobility rates . . . fell sharply over the
2000s. Thus, the colleges that may have offered many low-income
students pathways to success are becoming less accessible to
them."[86] As Chris Findeisen notes, for students coming from the
poorest quartile "the chances of graduating from college have
scarcely risen above 6%," leading him to point out that it is
safe to assume that the actual number of these students who enroll
in MFA programs is "very small."[87] Add to this that those who
get graduate degrees in the humanities are not very racially diverse. While the racial diversity of master's degree recipients has
been on the rise over the last twenty years, if slowly, from
25 percent of graduates who identified as other than white in 1995
to 36 percent in 2013, the MFA in creative writing went from only
12 percent of graduates who identified as other than white in 1995
to a minor increase of 18 percent in 2013.[88] This also points to how
U.S. literary production is limited to a fairly narrow demographic, not a mass one.

Just as I would be hesitant to understand the increasingly large
percentage of the U.S. population that receives a college degree
as indicative of an equitable system, I think the story of what happened to the independent magazine might suggest some additional reasons to be hesitant with understanding abundance as
equity. As I have been telling this story so far, the independent
magazine has been a battleground that has been friendly to
various forms of literary resistance, and the state in response
attempts in various ways to control or limit this resistance sometimes by starting their own magazines or co-opting existing
journals, at other times by censoring. And just as avant garde
modernism and the literatures associated with decolonization

announced their arrival through the form of the little magazine, so did the various sorts of movement literatures. The story of the Black Arts movement, for instance, cannot be told without considering journals such as *Umbra, Nommo, the Liberator, Black Dialogue,* and *Freedomways.* As Kalamu ya Salaam points out, "A major reason for the widespread dissemination and adoption of Black Arts was the development of nationally distributed magazines that printed manifestos and critiques in addition to offering publishing opportunities for a proliferation of young writers."[89] But it is not just the various factions of the Black Arts and Black Power movements, most literary movements or schools that existed in the last half of the twentieth century announced their presence through little magazines and journals. Bamboo Ridge, for instance, began as a workshop / support group and the journal *Bamboo Ridge.* It is hard to imagine language writing without *This, Tottel's,* and $L=A=N=G=U=A=G=E$. These journals, usually financed by the communities they represent, cultivate independent aesthetic or politicized literatures.

Then sometime around the turn of the century, the Association of Writers and Writing Programs put together a series of recommended guidelines, "Hallmarks of a Successful MFA Program in Creative Writing."[90] Among the hallmarks of a successful creative writing program is a literary journal or small press. And in years since the literary magazine has been "common"-ed, a huge number of literary magazines have been established, most of them glossy and institutionally supported but without a community of readers beyond their editors. These magazines were very different than the little magazines of modernism and various decolonization movements in that they tended to have a rotating editorial staff (usually students), existed mainly as a vehicle for professionalization, and often had as their reason for being not a political or aesthetic agenda but promotion of a degree program. Small Press Distribution, for instance, refuses to distribute any more literary magazines because the sales on them are so low (and sales that are too low for Small Press Distribution have to be fairly close to nonexistent). The glut of literary magazines has made it almost impossible for an intellectually meaningful readership to exist. So the little magazine lost both community need and support and arts funding at the same time due to its incorporation into the creative writing MFA system. Basically, the MFA managed to break the idea of a meaningful literary magazine in shorter order than the CIA. And if one believes Salaam that the independent magazine was crucial to the Black Arts movement or believes Bulson that the little magazine provided "an alternative model of the literary field that emerged during and after modernism, one that was *decommercialized, decapitalized,* and *decentered,*" then this matters.[91] But it is not just the magazine. The same can be said about the poetry reading and the literary gatherings. These spaces in the past have functioned as a sort of community-maintained commons, one that is permeable and decentralized. And when they move into higher education physically or when they are maintained outside of higher education only by those who have an MFA, certain demographics are dispossessed. This is just one more way that growth of the MFA and the idea that one should get an MFA to become a writer becomes a little less than the mild aesthetic project than McGurl admits.

By the end of the century, years of manipulation—that long history of the previous chapters—had severed literature's ties to resistance movements and it seemed there was no alternative to higher education (or the workshop form that it created). Even the organizations designed to rectify the inequities that were the result of this moment where writers seemed to come out of universities more often than not, ended up either mimicking or deeply embedded in higher education. June Jordan's "Poetry for the People" was one of the more successful examples of an institution that desired to be attentive to poetry's relationship to social movements. It resulted in an anthology and an extended pedagogical network. But it seems telling that when Jordan started it she did it at UC Berkeley and not at a community-run center in Oakland, that its mission had an "academic focus," that it aimed to bridge the gap between the university and the community.[92] I do not want to suggest that this is a failure on Jordan's part. She is someone who in the 1970s was tireless in her demands for open admissions. And UC Berkeley could for sure benefit from bridging some gaps it has with the community. Rather, I read it as an indication that things were structurally different at the turn of the century than they were in the 1970s. Even someone as attentive as Jordan was forced into a form of institutionalization that she spent much of her previous years questioning. Similarly, many of those thirty or so writers that I mentioned in that first section have similar stories of writing an autonomous literature within institutions. About half of those thirty or so writers I mentioned have an MFA (or if not an MFA, then a PhD). Many of their books have been published with university presses. And those who have published with a small or independent press, have done so with a literary one, usually one that exists because of government and foundation grants. There is no equivalent to something like Broadside, few moments where a political organization like Crusade for Justice publishes a book of poems as part of their struggle.

Often when I mention that poetry's alliances are different than they were in the 1970s, writers who are committed to the idea that poetry is a place for struggle point me to two possible exceptions. Sometimes they point me to a series of politically meaningful works that have gotten more attention in the last five years than politically meaningful works tend to get. Their examples vary. My own list of this sort of work would include but would not be in any way limited to Daniel Borzutzky's *The Performance of Being Human* (about the economic disparity between the United States and Latin America), Claudia Rankine's *Citizen* (about the continuing legacy of racism and also of police murder of black youth), Solmaz Sharif's *Look* (about America's invasions of Afghanistan and Iraq that uses words and phrases from *Department of Defense Dictionary of Military and Associated Terms*), Danez Smith's *Don't Call Us Dead* (about police violence against black men and also HIV), and Layli Long Soldier's *WHEREAS* (in part a response to the 2009 congressional resolution of apology to Native Americans). Rankine's *Citizen* is, of course, the breakthrough work here. And it is a sign that literature is being recognized more for its critique that this book, and not a collection of lyric poems about universal emotions, has become one of the defining books of the last five or so years.

In my defense, I would point out that I have never argued that meaningful work is not being written. In fact, my point is the opposite. It is that the structural conditions of production that define this moment limit the reach of political works. What concerns me about literary production in the United States at the turn of the twenty-first century is not literature itself, not its content or its aesthetic concerns, but the narrowing of the networks that support its publication and distribution, networks that in turn limit it to the mainly literary and isolate it from resistance movements, even though the content and the aesthetics of these works might have much to contribute. These works are all part of the very isolating institutionalization that I am talking about, not the reverse. Most of these books were published by Graywolf (only

Borzutzky's was not), a distinguished literary and independent—as in not of the marketplace (in 2016, about a two-thirds of Graywolf's revenue came from sales; the rest from various sorts of grants, fund-raising, and contributions) but also not a community nor a movement—press.[93] All of these writers came out of MFA programs. The audience for this work is institutional and professional.

The other often-mentioned exception is the more activist version of the literary nonprofit. These nonprofits usually run a series of low-cost or free workshops, organize readings, award prizes, and do other sorts of literary advocacy for underrepresented writers. The Asian American Writers' Workshop, "devoted to the creating, publishing, developing and disseminating of creative writing by Asian Americans," was one of the first as it formed in 1991.[94] And Cave Canem, with its desire "to remedy the under-representation and isolation of African American poets in the literary landscape," was formed five years later, in 1996.[95] A whole series of these sorts of organizations—Callaloo Creative Writing Workshops, VONA, Kundiman, Con Tinta, Canto Mundo, and Kimbilo—appeared at the turn of the twenty-first century. There are also any number of more localized examples of this sort of work.

These organizations are correctives to more establishment, and traditionally less racially attentive, literary institutions such as the Bread Loaf Writers' Conference or the Community of Writers at Squaw Valley or the Stegner Fellowship. And also corrective to how U.S. literary production in the aggregate is in no way racially representative (for another study I am working on with C. O. Grossman and Stephanie Young, we are finding that U.S. literary production is in the aggregate about 95 percent white).[96] And there is much to indicate that organizations like Cave Canem, as a sort of activist wing of the canon wars of the late 1990s, played a significant role in racially diversifying higher education's contemporary canon. For after the late 1990s, if U.S. population demographics are used as a measure, the writers that are invited to read on campus are racially diverse and a diverse range of writers tend to be taught in both the literature courses designed for MFA students and in more generic contemporary literature classes. Even State Department propaganda characterizes American literature as committed to diversity. "Literature in the United States today is likewise dazzlingly diverse, exciting, and evolving," Kathryn VanSpanckeren writes in the *Outline of American Literature*. She continues, "On a typical Sunday the list of best-selling books in the *New York Times Book Review* testifies to the extraordinary diversity of the current American literary scene."[97] (She is not really correct about the *New York Times Book Review*. Roxane Gay, for instance, notices that "nearly 90% of the books reviewed by *The New York Times* [were] written by white writers."[98] How to understand this insistence by institutions that U.S. literature is diverse, is a sort of social justice project, when it is not in the aggregate is something I am attempting to puzzle through.) But otherwise, VanSpanckeren is right; institutionally authorized U.S. literature is racially diverse.

Those who see these nonprofits as an exception to my observations often point to how they resemble the various racially separatist organizations that cultivated the resistant and autonomous movement literatures of the late 1960s and early 1970s. But there is a decidedly different rhetoric and relation to the institution that defines organizations like Cave Canem than, say, something like the Black Arts Repertory Theatre / School. When Baraka wrote about revolutionary theater he wrote, "The Revolutionary Theatre must Accuse and Attack anything that can be accused and attacked" and "We want actual explosions and actual brutality."[99] Cave Canem, in contradistinction, talks about their commitment to "the professional growth of African American poets."[100] Nearly all these twenty-first-century organizations share a rhetoric of professionalization. Websites note major prizes won, books published, MFA programs attended, and academic jobs. And even though they often reference a rhetoric of cultural uplift, they are organizations that argue for inclusion in existing organizations and support (rather than overturn) the institutionalization that defines contemporary literature production. Many of these programs are in some way loosely affiliated with or their programming housed in private colleges and universities. Kundiman and Cave Canem are regularly official Literary Partners of the Association of Writers and Writing Programs (which is interesting because the association is there to represent college and university writing programs, programs that have historically replaced these sorts of cultural projects).

I would never say that these organizations do not matter or are corrupt. Nor would I wish them away. But they are a part of and are formed by this era of institutionalization, not a resistance to it. Kenneth Warren goes harder and argues of these organizations that "the true story appears to be one of class consolidation within—rather than the economic democratization of—American society."[101] And there is a certain truth here. These nonprofits have not been able to diversify the unusual whiteness of U.S. literary production in the aggregate and neither have they been able to diversify economically who writes literature or counter the narrowing of its practitioners to those with degrees from top schools.

It may be that each time gets the literature that it deserves. Now is, after all, a different time than the turn of the previous century, than the late 1960s and early 1970s. It is a different time than when Du Bois sent his telegram. Different than when Jolas was editing *Transition*. Also different than the moment Washington describes in *The Other Blacklist*. And that is sort of my point. It is not that the government is actively suppressing literature. It does not have to do so. Literature has been sequestered into irrelevance. The FBI no longer has to develop files on writers because the terms on which literature is written, who it is written for, and where it is possible to write it have changed.

I tend to think of what happens to U.S. literature post-45 as a sort of dispossession of certain demographics from the commons of literature. While there are a thousand variations of community writing workshops on offer right now, none of them are anything like the various organizations of the 1930s—such as the American Artists' Congress, the Artists Union, and the Harlem Artists Guild—that were created to support the development of left, antifascist literature.

But at the same time, I do not want to suggest that there was some utopic prior moment where everyone thought of literature as a form that represented their concerns, told their stories. Or a moment when anyone could be a writer. Literature's concerns and who feels it might matter to them or feels they might be able to write it at any one moment has always been a complicated story with a long history. Literature has never been inclusive. If not dependent on the market, it has been dependent on the patronage of the rich; if not dependent on the rich, then on the state. However, as Casanova's book charts, it has long had a tradition of alternative networks and concerns. And within the last half of the century, as the gates and options for literary production have been narrowing, these have disappeared. Around 30 percent of the writers in issue number fourteen of Jolas's *Transition* were communists, Marxists, or some sort of fellow travelers. If I attempted to locate an equivalent to *Transition,* I might point to the journal *Lana Turner,* edited by David Lau and Cal Bedient. The most recent issue had perhaps eight writers who might be something other than a Democrat.

Two additional complications in this moment. One is that this is a moment where there has been an astronomical increase in the amount of literature published. Matthew Wilkens notes that after 2000, over 50,000 novels a year are published in the United States (prior to 2000 that number was less than 10,000). Books in Print lists close to a million books of fiction published in English in the United States between 2000 and 2017.

Then paradoxically, at the same time literary reading is in a free fall. Every few years there is a new study that announces this. The National Endowment for the Arts most recent "Annual Arts Basic Survey (2013–2015)" quantifies: "From 47 percent in 2012, literary reading rates fell to 45 percent in 2013, and to 43.1 percent in 2015."[102] In 2012, less than 7 percent of the population read a single poem in a year.[103] The Survey of Public Participation in the Arts also notes: "Since 2002, the share of poetry-readers has contracted by 45 percent—resulting in the steepest decline in participation in any literary genre."[104] Thomas Franssen and Giselinde Kuipers in "Sociology of Literature and Publishing in the Early 21st Century: Away from the Centre" also notice that currently a very small demographic of people actually read literature. They point out that as a result of "the centrifugal effects of globalization and regionalization," literature's central position has "given away to other, mainly visual and digital, cultural forms. In the process it has lost much of its political clout. Literature seems to pose little or no threat to those groups it may have previously worried, and is of little consequence to elites in the twenty-first century. Instead, it has become an object of cultural consumption, for dwindling and aging publics."[105] Again, the Survey of Public Participation in the Arts quantifies: "Sixty-five to 74-year-olds now are among those with the highest rates of literary reading."[106]

In this time, literary institutions, often the very ones responsible for separating literature from its ties to resistance movements, are free and easy with a Lorde-esque rhetoric. "Literature is a sanctuary" a recent statement from the University of Southern California English Department begins. And it continues, it is "through reading and writing, through identifying with characters who are nothing like us, we who love words learn to love others."[107] Artistic communities as they are currently configured can function as "an unbreakable bulwark against whoever would try to subvert the goodness of this great nation!" a piece on LitHub proclaims.[108] Harriett, the blog for the Poetry Foundation, publishes endless versions of these sorts of claims. At moments this rhetoric is indistinguishable from rhetoric used by the Congress for Cultural Freedom officials. And while it is not entirely a fair comparison, a lot of things get said about literature that no sane would person ever say about a number of other art forms that have mainly an aging and dwindling audience and that are dependent entirely on support from the state and the rich such as opera or chamber music or ballet. It is hard, for instance, to imagine someone arguing, as Paula Moya does in *The Social Imperative,* that "reading and teaching novels by socially subordinated people can provide a particularly rich context for learning about the interactions, institutions, and ideas that create and maintain different forms of inequality" about opera.[109] It is not necessarily that Moya is wrong. Literature has a long history of teaching about inequality. It just is in this current moment too dependent on those institutions that create and maintain in-equality to be a meaningful alternative to them.

Nowak in an interview with Phil Metres talks about litera-ture's limited reach, how even though his work addresses "dein-dustrialization and the collapse of certain sectors of the urban geography . . . [*Revenants*] was never able to enter into these larger conversations."[110] It is unsurprising that this observation is coming from Mark Nowak. He was an early critic of the institu-tionalization of creative writing brought on by the MFA, insis-tently juxtaposing it with "a historical model of radical writers workshops (the John Reed Clubs of the CPUSA, Ernesto Carde-nal's *talleres de poesia,* etc.)" pointing out that these were more tenable models for writing praxis and pedagogy than the "neo-liberal MFA industry."[111]

Like Nowak, I also feel this in the relation that my writing has to my hometown. I have written several times about southern Ohio, where I grew up, where I still have family, a place that de-fines me in many ways. I would echo Nowak that even as my writing is often about the large scale economic changes that some-thing like NAFTA brought to the region, my work has never been able to enter into the conversation of the region. I have never read in my hometown, not even within a hundred miles of it. My work is not sold there. My closest friends from the region barely know that I write literature. If they do, they see it as an idiosyn-cratic hobby. They do not see it as mattering to their attempts to understand what is happening to their ability to live, even though attempting to understand this is an increasingly necessary survival skill for those who still live there. The producers and the consumers of the sort of literature that I write are for the most part those, like myself, with a professional stake in its continuation.

There are all these things literature can do. But right now these things are limited by certain structural conditions. And beginning to understand why it cannot is one way to begin to cultivate these moments where literature is relevant and resistant. In the current state of things, it is hard to even notice these changes. As Siddhartha Deb writes, "The idealized image of the American writer remains that of the individual uncontaminated by pressure from state or society, their support for wars an entirely voluntary matter, their writing as well as their thinking formed in the crucible of a free society and a free market that rewards talent and independent thinking and demands no conformity in return." He continues, "This fiction of independence and innocence survives whatever insidious nexus between state and writer the historical record might offer."[112] To put this another way, just as Adorno's 1962 claim in "Commitment"—that committed literature takes but does not give—does not describe the relationship that various political movements at the time had to literature, it might also be that Lorde's claim—that poetry easily moves from language to tangible action—is not possible in the current moment.

Conclusion

I HAVE A FRIEND who jokes that most books of political theory have five chapters that describe a crisis and then a six page conclusion of Keynesian suggestions for reform that the analysis in the previous five chapters have suggested are useless. I have thought of this joke often as I worked on this conclusion. In these less than six pages, I will avoid reform. The more I worked on this study the harder it became for me to imagine any.

It was not for lack of trying. At a certain moment I began a simpleminded attempt to cultivate some possibility. As I am a writer, I am often asked to teach some sort of workshop. Usually these involve some reading assignments, some in class writing and sharing of writing. Trying to use this work to think about the ideas that provoked me to write this book, I developed one that I called "Poetry and the Police: Is a Resistant and / or Revolution-aligned Literature Possible? Could We Create One

Together? Would We Even Want To? If We Did, What Would We Do?" The reading list: Elisée Reclus's "Art and the People," the May 17, 1960, Situationist Manifesto, and Murray's "For a Revolutionary Culture."[1] These are very different works. Reclus's is a call for art that is so beautiful that it abolishes class: "The earth is infinitely beautiful, but for us to associate ourselves to its beauty, to glorify it by a respectful art, there is no other means but that of becoming free, of instituting the decisive revolution against money and of ennobling the class-struggle by abolishing the classes themselves."[2] The Situationists call for the seizure of UNESCO (it was written during the empire era of UNESCO, before the nations of the nonaligned movement began to revision the organization): "We propose an autonomous organization of the producers of the new culture, independent of the political and union organizations which currently exist, as we dispute their capacity to organize anything other than the management of that which already exists."[3] Murray, the same Murray of the San Francisco State University strike, argues that "our culture must not be something that the enemy enjoys, appreciates, or says is attractive, it must be repelling to the slave master. It must smash, shatter and crack his skull, crack his eyeballs, open and make water and gold dust run out."[4] Despite the disparate historical moments that influenced them, all imagine an art that is other than national, all presume that art can be autonomous in that it can separate itself from governmental forms of support and be in resistance. After discussing these works, I would attempt to next encourage the workshop to imagine revisiting this in our current moment: How might we free literature from these various forces I have been describing in this book? What would it look like to write some version of these works today? After three attempts at this workshop, I gave up. We could not do it.

I have thought of this book as a sort of auto-ethnographic project, an attempt to describe the way literature circulates in the very scenes in which I also circulate. I have been guilty at times of writing as if I have been visiting a foreign land, but this land is familiar. This story of how literary production has been increasingly institutionalized throughout the century is one I can also tell about myself. I went to college because of student loans. I became a poet because I went to college and took creative writing workshops. I went to graduate school because I went to college (it was a PhD in literature so those workshops were somewhat irrelevant to it but I went to graduate school because it felt like one possible way to be a poet in the world so maybe not). At graduate school, I co-edited a journal that I founded with Jena Osman because we had a commitment to literature that we thought of as autonomous but we started it with funds we got from the university. Almost all that I know about poetry I learned through higher education. Or nearby it. My second job was in a small college with a large MFA. There was, although I did not recognize it at the time, a bit of a hiring bubble in creative writing as institutions needed faculty to meet the growing student demand for creative writing workshops, a demand that was made possible at least partially by the 1992 Higher Education Amendments that expanded the lending possibilities of student loans. There I taught students how to write a politicized poetry at the same time that I taught them to enter institutions after graduation. My second and third books of poetry were also published by university presses.

I am also familiar with the State Department. An important mentor of mine, Robert Creeley, was included in *Writers on America*. A colleague and several other writers that I respect are also in the anthology. I have many friends who have studied at the International Writing Program. This story is also my story though in more specific ways. About halfway through writing this book, I was invited to do a weeklong workshop in Tijuana. My workshop, the organizer explained to me, would parallel a larger workshop that was being held for artists from Mexico and South America. The organizers were clear why they were inviting me: I was from the United States and there was apparently a fund that would only support bringing a U.S. artist to Mexico. And, the organizers added, while it would not be required, it would be great if I would be willing to donate my honorarium back to the program. There had been an earthquake, they explained, and the money that the Mexican government had committed to the preexisting workshop had been redirected. So my presence would not only provide some cash for the programming but they could also charge all of the housing for the Mexican and South American artists to the fund. (The housing was modest; a dorm that had been used to house women who worked in a massage parlor the year before the State Department began recommending that U.S. citizens not visit Tijuana; it was empty in 2010, as was all of Avenida Revolución.) When I finally got paid, I noticed the check was from the U.S. Department of Energy and had the slightly queasy realization that I had naively agreed to be a part of the of U.S. cultural diplomacy and not realized it.

I have also repeatedly thought about how much of the narrative that I tell about turn of the twenty-first century literature I could also tell about my own work. In the nineties, I wrote some works that used languages other than English. My second book of poems, *Fuck You-Aloha-I Love You,* used Pidgin and Hawaiian words. I did it for many of the reasons that I associate with those writers in the nineties. I lived in Hawaiʻi, a multilingual state, a place where writing in English felt very fraught. I felt that it was important to use these other languages, to acknowledge them. But these other languages disappeared from my work at the turn of the century. If I were a biographical self-critic, I could attribute this to moving from Hawai'i. But I moved to two places that also are richly multilingual and full of colonial histories, New York City and the Bay Area. So it is not that. I think there was, and is, something different in the aesthetic air. I continue to ask myself about this air and whether it, and my work, might also have been part of the turn to plain speech during the reign of Bush, although I would never care to think of it that way.

Still my intention in this book was not to just complain that literature is a genre that is unusually manipulated and dependent. It is to write a history of how it got that way. It is unclear to me how literature might be reclaimed from these institutions short of revolution. Not that I want to give in to what I have described. And yet I give in at every moment. Everything I have done in my life to get me out of this ecosystem has felt minor in impact.

Revolution though. There is some historical precedence that it is revolution that frees cultural production from the institutions that constantly work to contain it. Kristin Ross in *Communal Luxury* locates the beginnings of the Paris Commune not in the March 18, 1871, attempt by the formerly French but newly Prussian army to reclaim the armaments that failed but before that in the "popular reunions at the end of the Empire, the various associations and committees they spawned, and the 'buzzing hives' that were the revolutionary clubs of the Siege."[5] Robin D. G. Kelley notices something similar about the Watts riots. He notices that "a sense of revolt also found expression in a local arts movement dedicated to community self-determination."[6] That cultural production has not just a stubborn relationship to the nation but also to various sorts of resistance is not a new observation. But what I like about their observations is how sociological they are, how they are focused on where the culture and political discussions were happening. To return to Du Bois's telegram. He too was noticing this, noticing the importance of literature to the various anticolonial revolutions that were happening, noticing the buzzing hives, and also noticing the government's attempts to contain these hives.

We are for sure not there, yet. But one can always hope. For the buzzing hives are just a part of what Ross notices. She also notices that among the conditions that defined the creation of the Commune was that "the mid-nineteenth century and the years preceding the Commune was a moment not unlike our own, when artists feared increasingly for their livelihood."[7] She notices that more than two-thirds of graduates of the Ecole des Beaux Arts were unsuccessful at finding employment as an artist. It was these conditions that made the status of art and the artist such a focus of the Commune, that perpetuated the understanding that "art *lived*—not superfluous or trivial, but vital and indispensable to the community." Harney and Moten provide a similar glimmer of hope when they theorize the undercommons, the place that holds those who are marginal to the institution of higher education. Similar to Ross they point out that "the undercommons, its maroons, are always at war, always in hiding."[8] And then they conclude, "The uncanny feeling we are left with is that something else is there in the undercommons. It is the prophetic organization that works for the red and black abolition."[9] While it seems absurd at this moment, perhaps at some point in the near future, those current 60,000 holders of creative writing degrees (at least 59,000 of them unsuccessful at making a career in higher education) can make the status of art and the artist vital and indispensable to the community outside of the institutions that have claimed it into irrelevance.

NOTES

ACKNOWLEDGMENTS

INDEX

NOTES

Introduction

1. *The 1st International Conference of Negro Writers and Artists, Paris, Sorbonne, 19th–22nd September 1956* (Paris: Présence Africaine, 1956), 9.
2. At the time Du Bois oversaw an international group that opposed nuclear weapons and the U.S. State Department insisted that he register as a foreign agent. He refused to register, and even though he won the resulting trial, the government still rescinded his passport. He would not get it back until 1958 when the Supreme Court overturned the denial.
3. Joséphine Bouillon et al., "Messages," *Présence Africaine*, no. 8/10 (1956): 379–401. Capitalization and spelling as in original.
4. Guirdex Massé, "Cold War and Black Transnationalism: Aimé Césaire and Mercer Cook at the First International Congress of Black Writers and Artists," *Palimpsest: A Journal on Women, Gender, and the Black International* 4, no. 2 (2016): 115–34. James Baldwin and Chester Himes were also in attendance but not as delegates.
5. Hugh Wilford, *The Mighty Wurlitzer: How the CIA Played America* (Cambridge: Harvard University Press, 2009), 201–2.
6. Wilford, *Mighty Wurlitzer,* 201–2.

7. Hazel Rowley, *Richard Wright: The Life and Times* (Chicago: University of Chicago Press, 2008), 474.

8. Rowley, 474.

9. Rowley, 474.

10. James Campbell, *Exiled in Paris: Richard Wright, James Baldwin, Samuel Beckett and Others on the Left Bank* (Berkeley: University of California Press, 2003), 102.

11. Michael Fabre, *The World of Richard Wright* (Jackson: University Press of Mississippi, 1985), 206.

12. *1st International Conference*, 13.

13. *1st International Conference*, 217.

14. *1st International Conference*, 363, 367.

15. James Baldwin, "Princes and Powers," *Encounter*, no. 17 (1957): 52.

16. Theodor W. Adorno, *Notes to Literature*, trans. Shierry Weber Nicholsen, vol. 2 (New York: Columbia University Press, 1992), 93–94.

17. W. H. Auden, *Collected Poems* (New York: Vintage, 1991), 246.

18. Charles Bernstein, ed., *The Politics of Poetic Form: Poetry and Public Policy* (New York: Roof, 1990), 24.

19. Bernstein, 24.

20. Charles Bernstein, *Content's Dream: Essays, 1975–1984* (Evanston, IL: Northwestern University Press, 2001), 60.

21. Bernstein, *Politics of Poetic Form*, 212.

22. Christopher S. Nealon, *The Matter of Capital: Poetry and Crisis in the American Century* (Cambridge: Harvard University Press, 2011), 11.

23. Barrett Watten, "The Turn to Language and the 1960s," *Critical Inquiry* 29, no. 1 (2002): 148.

24. Ron Silliman, "Poetry and the Politics of the Subject," *Socialist Review* 88, no. 3 (1988): 63.

25. Dorothy Wang, *Thinking Its Presence: Form, Race, and Subjectivity in Contemporary Asian American Poetry* (Palo Alto, CA: Stanford University Press, 2013), 6.

26. Cynthia G. Franklin, Ruth Hsu, and Suzanne Kosanke, eds., *Navigating Islands and Continents: Conversations and Contestations in and Around the Pacific: Selected Essays* (Honolulu: University of Hawaii Press, 2000), 55.

27. James Smethurst, *The Black Arts Movement: Literary Nationalism in the 1960s and 1970s* (Chapel Hill: University of North Carolina Press, 2005), 148, 149.

28. T. S. Eliot, *On Poetry and Poets* (New York: Macmillan, 2009), 8.

29. Gloria Anzaldúa, *Borderlands / La Frontera: The New Mestiza* (San Francisco: Aunt Lute Books, 2007), 81.

30. Myung Mi Kim, *Commons* (Berkeley: University of California Press, 2002), 108.

31. Benedict Anderson, *Imagined Communities: Reflections on the Origin and Spread of Nationalism* (New York: Verso, 2006), 154.

32. Anderson, 145.

33. Pascale Casanova, *The World Republic of Letters* (Cambridge: Harvard University Press, 2004), 115.

34. Casanova, 279.

35. Alfred Arteaga, *Chicano Poetics: Heterotexts and Hybridities* (New York: Cambridge University Press, 1997), 9.

36. Smethurst, *Black Arts Movement,* 248.

37. Urayoan Noel, *In Visible Movement: Nuyorican Poetry from the Sixties to Slam* (Iowa City: University of Iowa Press, 2014), xix.

38. Robin D. G. Kelley, *Freedom Dreams: The Black Radical Imagination* (Boston: Beacon Press, 2003), 10.

39. Dale Smith, *Poets beyond the Barricade: Rhetoric, Citizenship, and Dissent After 1960* (Tuscaloosa: University of Alabama Press, 2012), 33.

40. Audre Lorde, *Sister Outsider: Essays and Speeches* (Emeryville, CA: Potter / TenSpeed / Harmony, 2012), 37.

41. Adorno, *Notes to Literature,* 2:93–94.

42. Benedict Anderson, *Imagined Communities: Reflections on the Origin and Spread of Nationalism* (Brooklyn, NY: Verso, 2006), 34.

43. Karl Marx and Friedrich Engels, *Karl Marx, Frederick Engels: Collected Works* (New York: International Publishers, 1994), 448.

44. Dave Beech, *Art and Value: Art's Economic Exceptionalism in Classical, Neoclassical and Marxist Economics* (Leiden: Brill, 2015), 23.

45. Beech, 23.

46. Andrew Goldstone, *Fictions of Autonomy: Modernism from Wilde to de Man* (New York: Oxford University Press, 2013).

47. Marc Shell and Werner Sollors, *Multilingual Anthology of American Literature: A Reader of Original Text with English Translations* (New York: New York University Press, 2000); Mary Louise Pratt, *Imperial Eyes: Travel Writing and Transculturation* (New York: Routledge, 1992); Doris Sommer, *Proceed with Caution, When Engaged by Minority Writing in the Americas* (Cambridge: Harvard University Press, 1999).

48. Gavin Jones, *Strange Talk: The Politics of Dialect Literature in Gilded Age America* (Berkeley: University of California Press, 1999), 37.

49. Bryan Wagner, *Disturbing the Peace: Black Culture and the Police Power after Slavery* (Cambridge: Harvard University Press, 2009), 20.

50. Jones, *Strange Talk*, 11.

51. Evan Kindley, *Poet-Critics and the Administration of Culture* (Cambridge: Harvard University Press, 2017), 16.

52. Subramanian Shankar, *Flesh and Fish Blood: Postcolonialism, Translation, and the Vernacular* (Berkeley: University of California Press, 2012), xv.

53. Jacques Derrida, *Monolingualism of the Other, Or, The Prosthesis of Origin* (Palo Alto, CA: Stanford University Press, 1998), 1, 3.

54. Rey Chow, *Not Like a Native Speaker: On Languaging as a Postcolonial Experience* (New York: Columbia University Press, 2014).

55. Matthew Hart and Jim Hansen, "Introduction: Contemporary Literature and the State," *Contemporary Literature* 49, no. 4 (2008): 506.

1. Turn of the Twenty-First Century: A Possible Literature of Resistance

1. Alastair Pennycook, *The Cultural Politics of English as an International Language* (Harlow, UK: Pearson, 1994), 14.

2. David Crystal, *Language Death* (New York: Cambridge University Press, 2002), 19.

3. Karin Wiecha, "New Estimates on the Rate of Global Language Loss," *The Rosetta Project: A Long Now Foundation Library of Human Languages* (blog), March 28, 2013, http://rosettaproject.org/blog/02013/mar/28/new-estimates-on-rate-of-language-loss/.

4. Lenore A. Grenoble and Lindsay J. Whaley, eds., *Endangered Languages: Language Loss and Community Response* (New York: Cambridge University Press, 1998); Daniel Nettle and Suzanne Romaine, *Vanishing Voices: The Extinction of the World's Languages* (New York: Oxford University Press, 2002); Mark Abley, *Spoken Here: Travels among Threatened Languages* (Boston: Houghton Mifflin Harcourt, 2003); Christopher Moseley, ed., *Encyclopedia of the World's Endangered Languages* (London: Routledge, 2007); K David Harrison, *When Languages Die: The Extinction of the World's Languages and the Erosion of Human Knowledge* (New York: Oxford University Press, 2008);

Nicholas Evans, *Dying Words: Endangered Languages and What They Have to Tell Us* (Hoboken, NJ: Wiley-Blackwell, 2009).

5. Julie Siebens and Tiffany Julian, "Native North American Languages Spoken at Home in the United States and Puerto Rico: 2006–2010" (Washington, DC: U.S. Census Bureau, December 2011), http://www .census.gov/prod/2011pubs/acsbr10–10.pdf; M. Paul Lewis, Gary F. Simons, and Charles D. Fennig, eds., *Ethnologue: Languages of the World*, 19th edition (2016), www.ethnologue.com/19.

6. Elizabeth M. Grieco et al., "The Size, Place of Birth, and Geographic Distribution of the Foreign-Born Population in the United States: 1960 to 2010" (Washington, DC: U.S. Census Bureau, October 2012), http:// citeseerx.ist.psu.edu/viewdoc/download?doi=10.1.1.305.3351&rep =rep1&type=pdf.

7. "U.S. Foreign-Born Population Trends," *Pew Research Center's Hispanic Trends Project* (blog), September 28, 2015, http://www.pewhispanic.org /2015/09/28/chapter-5-u-s-foreign-born-population-trends/.

8. Hyon B. Shin, "Language Use and English-Speaking Ability: 2000" (Washington, DC: U.S. Census Bureau, October 2003), https://www .census.gov/prod/2003pubs/c2kbr-29.pdf.

9. Camille Ryan, "Language Use in the United States: 2011" (Washington, DC: U.S. Census Bureau, August 2013), https://www.census.gov/prod /2013pubs/acs-22.pdf.

10. Claude Hagège, *On the Death and Life of Languages* (New Haven, CT: Yale University Press, 2009), 119.

11. The summary of legislation about the English language that follows is indebted to James Crawford's *Hold Your Tongue: Bilingualism and the Politics of "English Only"* (Boston: Addison-Wesley, 1993) and *At War with Diversity: U.S. Language Policy in an Age of Anxiety* (Bristol, UK: Multilingual Matters, 2000).

12. Anne Tardos, *Uxudo* (Berkeley, CA: Tuumba Press, 1999).

13. Mark Nowak, *Revenants* (Minneapolis: Coffee House Press, 2000).

14. Judy Halebsky, *Space/Gap/Interval/Distance* (San Francisco: Sixteen Rivers Press, 2012).

15. Padcha Tuntha-obas, *Trespasses* (Berkeley, CA: O Books, 2006).

16. Rodolfo Gonzales, *I Am Joaquin: An Epic Poem* (Denver, CO: R. Gonzales, 1967); Alurista, *Nationchild Plumaroja, 1969–1972* (San Diego: Toltecas en Aztlán, 1972); Juan Felipe Herrera, *Rebozos of Love//We Have Woven//Sudor de Pueblos//On Our Back: Cantos* (San Diego: Toltecas en Aztlán, 1974).

17. Gloria Anzaldúa, *Borderlands/La Frontera: The New Mestiza* (San Francisco: Aunt Lute Books, 2007), 81, and *The All-Union Day of the Shock Worker* (New York: Roof Books, 2001), 109.

18. Hugo García Manríquez, *Anti-Humboldt: A Reading of the North American Free Trade Agreement* (New York: Litmus Press, 2014).

19. Francisco Alarcón, *Snake Poems: An Aztec Invocation* (San Francisco: Chronicle Books, 1992), 154.

20. Cecilia Vicuña, *Unravelling Words and Weaving Water* (Minneapolis: Graywolf Press, 1992).

21. Jozuf Hadley, *Chalukyu Eensai: Three Poems in Pidgin English* (Honolulu: Sandwich Islands, 1972).

22. Darrell H. Y. Lum, *Sun: Short Stories and Drama* (Honolulu: Bamboo Ridge Press, 1980).

23. Eric Chock, *Last Days Here* (Honolulu: Bamboo Ridge Press, 1990); Lois-Ann Yamanaka, *Saturday Night at the Pahala Theatre* (Honolulu: Bamboo Ridge Press, 1993); Lee A. Tonouchi, *Da Word* (Honolulu: Bamboo Ridge Press, 2001); Kathy Dee Kaleokealoha Kaloloahilani Banggo, *4-Evaz, Anna* (Honolulu: Tinfish Press, 1997); Lisa Linn Kanae, *Sista Tongue* (Honolulu: Tinfish Press, 2001).

24. Diane Glancy, *Lone Dog's Winter Count* (New York: West End Press, 1991); Diane Glancy, *The Voice That Was in Travel: Stories* (Norman: University of Oklahoma Press, 1999).

25. Guillermo Gómez-Peña, *Warrior for Gringostroika: Essays, Performance Texts, and Poetry* (Minneapolis: Graywolf Press, 1993).

26. Robert Sullivan, *Star Waka: Poems by Robert Sullivan* (Auckland: Auckland University Press, 1999).

27. James Thomas Stevens and Caroline Sinavaiana, *Mohawk/Samoa: Transmigrations* (Honolulu: Subpress, 2005).

28. James Thomas Stevens, *Tōkinish* (New York: First Intensity, 1994).

29. James Thomas Stevens, *Bulle/Chimére* (Lawrence, KS: First Intensity Press, 2006), n.p.

30. Haunani-Kay Trask, *Light in the Crevice Never Seen* (Corvallis, OR: Calyx Books, 1999); Haunani-Kay Trask, *Night Is a Sharkskin Drum* (Honolulu: University of Hawaii Press, 2002).

31. Alani Apio, *Kāmau* (Honolulu: Palila Books, 1998); Alani Apio, *Kāmau A'e* (Honolulu: Kumu Kahua Theater Co., 1998).

32. Teresia Kieuea Teaiwa, *Searching for Nei Nim'anoa* (Suva, Fiji: Mana Publications, 1995), ix.

33. Kristin Naca, *Bird Eating Bird* (New York: Harper Collins, 2009).

34. M. NourbeSe Philip, *She Tries Her Tongue, Her Silence Softly Breaks* (Charlottetown, Prince Edward Island: Ragweed Press, 1989).

35. M. NourbeSe Philip, *Zong!* (Middletown, CT: Wesleyan, 2011).

36. Walter K. Lew, *Excerpts from: Δikth/ 딕테/ 딕티/DIKTE for DICTEE* (Seoul: Yeul Publishing Company, 1992).

37. Cathy Park Hong, *Dance Dance Revolution: Poems* (New York: W. W. Norton, 2007).

38. Jonathan Stalling, *Yingelishi: Sinophonic English Poetry and Poetics* (Denver: Counterpath Press, 2011).

39. Myung Mi Kim, *Commons* (Berkeley: University of California Press, 2002), 110.

40. Chris Chen, "Uncommon Measure: The Poetics of Comparative Racialization in Myung Mi Kim's Dura," unpublished manuscript.

41. Myung Mi Kim, *Dura* (New York: Nightboat Books, 2008), 12, 75.

42. Kim, 20, 21, 22.

43. Kim, 68.

44. David R. White, Lise Friedman, and Tia Levinson, *Poor Dancer's Almanac: Managing Life and Work in the Performing Arts* (Durham, NC: Duke University Press, 1993), 272.

45. Gómez-Peña, *Warrior for Gringostroika,* 43.

46. James Thomas Stevens, *A Bridge Dead in the Water* (Cromer, UK: Salt Publishing, 2007), 1.

47. Cecilia Vicuña, *Instan* (Berkeley, CA: Kelsey Street Press, 2002).

48. Myung Mi Kim, *Under Flag* (Berkeley, CA: Kelsey Street Press, 1998), 29.

49. Myung Mi Kim, *The Bounty* (Tucson: Chax Press, 1996), 25.

50. Kim, *Dura,* 79.

51. Benedict Anderson, *Imagined Communities: Reflections on the Origin and Spread of Nationalism* (New York: Verso, 2006), 32.

52. Trask, *Night Is a Sharkskin Drum,* 63.

53. Teaiwa, *Searching for Nei Nim'anoa,* 80–81.

54. Tonouchi, *Da Word,* 130.

55. Yamanaka, *Saturday Night at the Pahala Theatre,* 41.

56. Noelani Arista, "I Ka Mo'olelo Nō Ke Ola: In History There Is Life," *Anglistica* 15, no. 2 (2011): 17.

57. See Sam L. No'eau Warner, "The Movement to Revitalize Hawaiian Language and Culture," in *The Green Book of Language Revitalization in Practice: Toward a Sustainable World,* eds. Leanne Hinton and Ken Hale

(Abingdon-on-Thames, UK: Brill, 2001) for a good summary of these changes.

58. "A Timeline of Revitalization | Aha Punana Leo," accessed January 18, 2013, http://www.ahapunanaleo.org/index.php?/about/a_timeline_of _revitalization/.

59. See Charlene Sato's "Sociolinguistic Variation and Language Attitudes in Hawaii," in *English around the World: Sociolinguistic Perspectives,* ed. Jenny Cheshire (New York: Cambridge University Press, 1991), 647–63.

60. "Pidgin and Education," accessed January 18, 2013, http://www.hawaii .edu/sls/pidgin.html.

61. See, for instance, Lee A. Tonouchi, *Da Kine Dictionary* (Honolulu: Bess Press, 2005), and *Pidgin to Da Max* (Honolulu: Bess Press, 1981).

62. Kanae, *Sista Tongue;* Cynthia G. Franklin, Ruth Hsu, and Suzanne Kosanke, *Navigating Islands and Continents: Conversations and Contestations in and around the Pacific: Selected Essays* (Honolulu: University of Hawaii Press, 2000).

63. Rodney Morales, "Literature," in *Multicultural Hawai'i: The Fabric of a Multiethnic Society,* ed. Michael Haas, 1998, 125.

64. Richard Hamasaki, ed., *Anthology Hawaii: Seaweeds and Constructions* (Honolulu: Elepaio Press, 1979); Dana Naone, ed., *Malama: Hawaiian Land and Water* (Honolulu: Bamboo Ridge Press, 1985); Joseph P. Balaz, ed., *Ho'omanoa; An Anthology of Contemporary Hawaiian Literature* (Honolulu: Ku Pa'a, 1989).

65. Rob Wilson, *Reimagining the American Pacific: From South Pacific to Bamboo Ridge and Beyond* (Durham, NC: Duke University Press, 2000), 119.

66. Dennis Carroll, "Hawai'i's 'Local' Theatre," *TDR: The Drama Review* 44, no. 2 (2000): 147.

67. Carroll, "Hawai'i's 'Local' Theatre," 147.

68. Apio, *Kāmau A'e,* 5.

69. Apio, *Kāmau A'e,* 5.

70. Noenoe K. Silva, *Aloha Betrayed: Native Hawaiian Resistance to American Colonialism* (Durham, NC: Duke University Press, 2004), 134.

71. Pascale Casanova, *The World Republic of Letters* (Cambridge: Harvard University Press, 2004), 116.

72. Roger Williams, *A Key into the Language of America* (Carlisle, MA: Applewood Books, 1997).

73. Hernando Ruiz de Alarcón, *Treatise on the Heathen Superstitions: That Today Live among the Indians Native to This New Spain 1629* (Norman: University of Oklahoma Press, 1987).

74. "James Thomas Stevens | IAIA," accessed July 15, 2014, http://www.iaia .edu/academics/degree-programs/creative-writing/faculty/james-stevens/.

75. Rosmarie Waldrop, *A Key into the Language of America* (New York: New Directions Publishing, 1994), xx.

76. Alarcón, *Snake Poems,* back cover.

77. Alfred Arteaga, *Chicano Poetics: Heterotexts and Hybridities* (New York: Cambridge University Press, 1997), 8.

78. M. M. Bakhtin, *The Dialogic Imagination: Four Essays* (Austin: University of Texas Press, 2010).

79. Patricia E. Rubertone, *Grave Undertakings* (Washington, DC: Smithsonian, 2001), 42.

80. Williams, *A Key into the Language of America.*

81. Alarcón, *Snake Poems,* back cover.

82. Michael Berube, "Introduction: Worldly English," *MFS Modern Fiction Studies* 48, no. 1 (2002): 3.

83. Apio, *Kāmau A'e,* 40.

84. Franklin, Hsu, and Kosanke, *Navigating Islands and Continents,* 55.

85. Trask, *Light in the Crevice Never Seen,* 67.

86. "Hookupu Master Plan," *Ka Lahui Hawaii* (blog), October 7, 2009, 3, https://kalahuihawaii.wordpress.com/hookupu/.

87. "Hookupu Master Plan," 19.

88. David Graeber, *Possibilities: Essays on Hierarchy, Rebellion and Desire* (Oakland, CA: AK Press, 2007).

2. Stubborn Nationalism: Example One, Avant Garde Modernism

1. Charles Bernstein, *Content's Dream: Essays, 1975–1984* (Evanston, IL: Northwestern University Press, 2001), 246.

2. Angie Maxwell, *The Indicted South: Public Criticism, Southern Inferiority, and the Politics of Whiteness* (Chapel Hill: University of North Carolina Press, 2014), 89.

3. Claude McKay, *Songs of Jamaica* (London: Aston W. Gardner, 1912), 5.

4. Robert Lowell, "Robert Lowell Accepts the 1960 National Book Award for Poetry for Life Studies, The National Book Foundation," accessed March 14, 2013, http://www.nationalbook.org/nbaacceptspeech_rlowell

.html#.UUFLxjckTkd; Ron Silliman, "Silliman's Blog," December 27, 2003, http://ronsilliman.blogspot.com/2003/12/one-of-gifts-i-got-for -christmas-this.html.

5. Peter Quartermain, *Disjunctive Poetics: From Gertrude Stein and Louis Zukofsky to Susan Howe* (New York: Cambridge University Press, 1992).

6. Gauri Viswanathan, *Masks of Conquest: Literary Study and British Rule in India* (New York: Columbia University Press, 2014), 10.

7. Bill Ashcroft, Gareth Griffiths, and Helen Tiffin, *The Empire Writes Back: Theory and Practice in Post-Colonial Literatures* (Abingdon-on-Thames: Routledge, 2002), 4.

8. Frantz Fanon, *The Wretched of the Earth* (New York: Grove Press, 1965).

9. Virginia Woolf, *Mr. Bennett and Mrs. Brown* (London: Hogarth Press, 1924), 4.

10. Woolf, 5.

11. Woolf, 20.

12. Gertrude Stein, *Lectures in America* (Boston: Beacon Press, 1935), 46.

13. Thomas Stearns Eliot, "War-Paint and Feathers," *Athenaeum* (1919): 122.

14. Thomas Stearns Eliot, *The Use of Poetry and the Use of Criticism: Studies in the Relation of Criticism to Poetry in England* (Cambridge: Harvard University Press, 1986), 155.

15. David E. Chinitz, *T. S. Eliot and the Cultural Divide* (Chicago: University of Chicago Press, 2005), 77.

16. T. S. Eliot, *On Poetry and Poets* (New York: Macmillan, 2009), 8.

17. Aimé Césaire, "The Man of Culture and His Responsibilities," *Présence Africaine* 24–25 (May 1959): 127.

18. Michael Richardson and Krzysztof Fijałkowski, *Refusal of the Shadow: Surrealism and the Caribbean* (New York: Verso, 1996), 126.

19. Richardson and Fijałkowski, 126.

20. Michael Goebel, *Anti-Imperial Metropolis: Interwar Paris and the Seeds of Third World Nationalism* (New York: Cambridge University Press, 2015), 4.

21. Brent Hayes Edwards, "The Shadow of Shadows," *Positions* 11, no. 1 (2003): 11–49.

22. Alec Hargreaves and Mark McKinney, *Post-Colonial Cultures in France* (Abingdon-on-Thames: Routledge, 2013), 8.

23. Tyler Stovall, "National Identity and Shifting Imperial Frontiers: Whiteness and the Exclusion of Colonial Labor after World War I," *Representations* 84, no. 1 (2003): 53.

24. Simon Gikandi, "Preface: Modernism in the World," *Modernism/Modernity* 13, no. 3 (2006): 421.

25. Robert Scholes and Clifford Wulfman, *Modernism in the Magazines: An Introduction* (New Haven: Yale University Press, 2010).

26. Eric Bulson, *Little Magazine, World Form* (New York: Columbia University Press, 2016), 1.

27. This is a different journal than the CIA front journal of the same name that I mention in the introduction.

28. Eugene Jolas, "Race and Language," *Transition: An International Quarterly for Creative Experiment,* no. 24 (June 1936): 112.

29. Eugène Jolas and Elliot Paul, "A Review," *Transition: An International Quarterly for Creative Experiment,* no. 12 (March 1928): 144.

30. Victor Llona, "Foreigners Writing in French," *Transition: An International Quarterly for Creative Experiment,* no. 2 (May 1927): 169.

31. Northrop Frye, *Fearful Symmetry: A Study of William Blake* (Princeton: Princeton University Press, 1947); Cleanth Brooks, *The Well Wrought Urn: Studies in the Structure of Poetry* (New York: Harcourt, 1947); William Kurtz Wimsatt, *The Verbal Icon: Studies in the Meaning of Poetry* (Lexington: University Press of Kentucky, 1954).

32. Michael North, *The Dialect of Modernism: Race, Language, and Twentieth-Century Literature* (New York: Oxford University Press, 1998), 63.

33. Kamau Brathwaite, *History of the Voice: The Development of Nation Language in Anglophone Caribbean Poetry* (Boston: New Beacon Books, 1984), 14.

34. Walter J. Ong, *Orality and Literacy* (Abingdon-on-Thames: Routledge, 2013), 39.

35. Ong, 36.

36. Gertrude Stein, "An Instant Answer or a Hundred Prominent Men," *Transition* 13 (1928): 118.

37. Stein, 118.

38. Ong, *Orality and Literacy,* 38; Gertrude Stein, "Made a Mile Away," *Transition* 8 (November 1927): 155.

39. Ong, *Orality and Literacy,* 38; Gertrude Stein, *Reflection on the Atomic Bomb* (Boston: Black Sparrow Press, 1973), 130, 131, 132, 135.

40. Gertrude Stein, "Studies in Conversation," *Transition: An International Quarterly for Creative Experiment,* no. 6 (September 1927): 77.

41. "An Elucidation," *Transition* 1 (June 1927): 64. See Ulla Dydo's *Gertrude Stein: The Language that Rises: 1923–1934* (Evanston, IL: Northwestern University Press, 2003) for a discussion of the publication of this piece. The *Transition* version has some key errors that make the piece even more

difficult to understand. *Transition* eventually published a corrected version of this piece in pamphlet form.

42. Stein, "Studies in Conversation," 75.

43. Gertrude Stein, "If He Thinks: A Novelette of Desertion," *Transition* 10, (January 1928): 12.

44. Stein, 13.

45. Marjorie Perloff, *Poetics in a New Key: Interviews and Essays* (Chicago: University of Chicago Press, 2014), 147.

46. Gertrude Stein, *Tender Buttons* (New York: Claire Marie, 1914), 10.

47. Stein, 51.

48. Stein, 20.

49. Stein, 48.

50. Stein, 45.

51. Stein, 45.

52. Stein, 9, 50, 21.

53. Stein, 63.

54. William Butler Yeats, *The Collected Poems of W. B. Yeats* (Ware, UK: Wordsworth Editions, 2000), 158; Thomas Stearns Eliot, *The Waste Land: A Facsimile and Transcript of the Original Drafts, Including the Annotations of Ezra Pound* (New York: Houghton Mifflin Harcourt, 1974), 88.

55. Edith Sitwell, *Poetry and Criticism* (New York: Henry Holt, 1926), 30.

56. Max Eastman, "Non-Communicative Art," *The Freeman* 4, no. 16 (1954): 574.

57. Laura Riding, "The New Barbarism, and Gertrude Stein," *Transition: An International Quarterly for Creative Experiment* 3 (June 1927): 157.

58. Gertrude Stein, *Gertrude Stein's America,* ed. Gilbert A. Harrison (New York: Liveright, 1996), 19.

59. Christian Thorne, "The Sea Is Not a Place; or, Putting the World Back into World Literature," *Boundary* 2 40, no. 2 (2013): 58, https://doi.org/10.1215/01903659–2151803.

60. Max Frankel, "Ex-Official of C.I.A. Lists Big Grants to Labor Aides," *New York Times,* May 8, 1967.

61. Frances Stonor Saunders, *The Cultural Cold War: The CIA and the World of Arts and Letters* (New York: New Press, 2013), 1.

62. Serge Guilbaut, *How New York Stole the Idea of Modern Art* (Chicago: University of Chicago Press, 1985); Penny Marie Von Eschen, *Satchmo Blows Up the World: Jazz Ambassadors Play the Cold War* (Cambridge: Harvard University Press, 2004).

63. Geoff Eley, *Forging Democracy: The History of the Left in Europe, 1850–2000* (New York: Oxford University Press, 2002), 206.

64. Lynn Mally, *Culture of the Future: The Proletkult Movement in Revolutionary Russia* (Berkeley: University of California Press, 1990), 68.

65. Mally, 33.

66. V. I. Lenin, "Party Organisation and Party Literature," in *Collected Works,* trans. Andrew Rothstein, vol. 10 (Moscow: Progress Publishers, 1962), 48–49, https://www.marxists.org/archive/lenin/works/1905/nov/13.htm.

67. Bengt Jangfeldt, *Mayakovsky: A Biography* (Chicago: University of Chicago Press, 2014).

68. Maksim Gorky et al., *Soviet Writers' Congress 1934: The Debate on Socialist Realism and Modernism in the Soviet Union* (London: Lawrence and Wishart, 1977), 154.

69. Greg Barnhisel, *Cold War Modernists: Art, Literature, and American Cultural Diplomacy* (New York: Columbia University Press, 2015), 28.

70. Michael Denning, *The Cultural Front: The Laboring of American Culture in the Twentieth Century* (New York: Verso, 2010), 46.

71. Denning, 45–46.

72. Saunders, *Cultural Cold War,* 118–19.

73. Greg Barnhisel, "Perspectives USA and the Cultural Cold War: Modernism in Service of the State," *Modernism/Modernity* 14, no. 4 (2007): 146.

74. Ellen Noonan, *The Strange Career of Porgy and Bess: Race, Culture, and America's Most Famous Opera* (Chapel Hill: University of North Carolina Press, 2012), 193.

75. Saunders, *Cultural Cold War,* 113.

76. Eric Bennett, *Workshops of Empire: Stegner, Engle, and American Creative Writing during the Cold War* (Iowa City: University of Iowa Press, 2015), 69.

77. Deborah N. Cohn, *The Latin American Literary Boom and U.S. Nationalism during the Cold War* (Nashville: Vanderbilt University Press, 2012), 29.

78. Saunders, *Cultural Cold War;* Peter Benson, *Black Orpheus, Transition, and Modern Cultural Awakening in Africa* (Berkeley: University of California Press, 1986); Petrus Cornelius Swanepoel, *Really Inside BOSS: A Tale of South Africa's Late Intelligence Service (and Something about the CIA)* (Pretoria: Piet Swanepoel, 2007); Cassandra Pybus, "CIA as Culture

Vultures," *Jacket2*, July 2000, http://jacketmagazine.com/12/pybus-quad
.html.

79. Saunders, *Cultural Cold War;* Patrick Iber, "Literary Magazines for
    Socialists Funded by the CIA, Ranked," *The Awl*, August 24, 2015,
    https://theawl.com/literary-magazines-for-socialists-funded-by-the-cia
    -ranked-93e65a5a710a.

80. Saunders, *Cultural Cold War,* 26.

81. Joel Whitney, *Finks: How the CIA Tricked the World's Best Writers* (New
    York: OR Books, 2017), 34.

82. Saunders, *Cultural Cold War,* 327.

83. George Watson, "Elegy for a Cold Warrior: Melvin Lasky 1920–2004,"
    Sewanee Review 115, no. 4 (2007): 649–54.

84. Whitney, *Finks,* 85.

85. Kathleen D. McCarthy, "From Cold War to Cultural Development: The
    International Cultural Activities of the Ford Foundation, 1950–1980,"
    Daedalus 116, no. 1 (1987): 96.

86. Whitney, *Finks,* 42.

87. Barnhisel, *Cold War Modernists,* 212.

88. As quoted in Whitney, *Finks,* 39.

89. Casanova, *World Republic of Letters,* 43.

90. Ian S. MacNiven, *"Literchoor Is My Beat": A Life of James Laughlin,
    Publisher of New Directions* (New York: Farrar, Straus and Giroux, 2014),
    286.

91. "'Bread or Freedom': The Congress for Cultural Freedom, the CIA, and
    the Arabic Literary Journal Ḥiwār (1962–67)," *Journal of Arabic Literature*
    44 (n.d.): 89.

92. Hazel Rowley, *Richard Wright: The Life and Times* (Chicago: University of
    Chicago Press, 2008), 474.

93. Whitney, *Finks,* 36–37.

94. James Campbell, *Talking at the Gates: A Life of James Baldwin,* new ed.
    (Berkeley: University of California Press, 1991).

95. Douglas Field, *A Historical Guide to James Baldwin* (New York: Oxford
    University Press, 2009), 7.

96. Richard Green, "Hollywood Roundtable," *The Unwritten Record* (blog),
    September 21, 2012, https://unwritten-record.blogs.archives.gov/2012/09
    /21/hollywood-roundtable/.

97. Nicholas Brown, *Utopian Generations: The Political Horizon of Twentieth-
    Century Literature* (Princeton: Princeton University Press, 2005), 3.

98. Keith Smith, "Library Trends," *Library Trends* 27 (Spring 1978): 469.

99. Brian Russell Roberts and Keith Foulcher, *Indonesian Notebook: A Sourcebook on Richard Wright and the Bandung Conference* (Durham, NC: Duke University Press, 2016), 17.

100. Richard Wright, *The Color Curtain: A Report on the Bandung Conference* (New York: World Publishing Company, 1956).

101. Peter Kalliney, "Modernism, African Literature, and the Cold War," *Modern Language Quarterly* 76, no. 3 (2015): 333–68.

102. Ulli Beier, *Decolonising the Mind: The Impact of the University on Culture and Identity in Papua New Guinea, 1971–1974* (Canberra, AU: Pandanus Books, 2005).

103. Albert S. Gérard, *European-Language Writing in Sub-Saharan Africa* (Amsterdam: John Benjamins Publishing, 1986), 670.

104. Aimé Césaire, "Culture and Colonisation," in *The 1st International Conference of Negro Writers and Artists, Paris, Sorbonne, 19th–22nd September 1956*, 193–207, quote on 197.

105. *1st International Conference*, 58.

106. "Facilitative Assistance Festac," Wikileaks Public Library of US Diplomacy (Department of State, September 2, 1976), https://search.wikileaks .org/plusd/cables/1976STATE217675_b.html; "Nigeria: Nobel Laureate Wole Soyinka Arrested, Meets with Cg," Wikileaks Public Library of US Diplomacy (Nigeria Lagos, May 20, 2004), https://search.wikileaks.org /plusd/cables/04LAGOS1068_a.html; "Soyinka Willing to Appeal to Hostage Takers," Wikileaks Public Library of US Diplomacy (Nigeria Lagos, March 17, 2006), https://search.wikileaks.org/plusd/cables /06LAGOS400_a.html; "Press Report: The Citizen Reports on Us-Sa," Wikileaks Public Library of US Diplomacy (South Africa Johannesburg, July 21, 1977), https://wikileaks.org/plusd/cables/1977JOHANN01862_c .html.

107. Benson, *Black Orpheus*, 57.

108. Benson, 29.

109. Kalliney, "Modernism,."

110. Onuora E. Nwuneli, "The Rise and Fall of Transition Magazine" (University of Wisconsin, Madison, 1970).

111. Rajat Neogy and Tony Hall, "Rajat Neogy on the CIA," *Transition* 32 (1967): 45–46; Nwuneli, "The Rise and Fall of Transition Magazine"; Swanepoel, *Really Inside BOSS*.

112. Benson, *Black Orpheus*.

113. Holt, "'Bread or Freedom,'" 89.

114. Nwuneli, "The Rise and Fall of Transition Magazine," 48.

115. Kalliney, "Modernism," 338.

116. "Prof. Ezekiel Mphahlele," Wikileaks Public Library of US Diplomacy (South Africa Pretoria, October 28, 1977), https://wikileaks.org/plusd /cables/1977PRETOR05796_c.html.

117. Wilford, *Mighty Wurlitzer,* 213.

118. F. Abiola Irele and Simon Gikandi, eds., *The Cambridge History of African and Caribbean Literature,* vol. 2 (Cambridge: Cambridge University Press, 2000).

119. Kalliney, "Modernism," 349.

120. Obiajunwa Wali, "The Dead End of African Literature?" *Transition,* no. 10 (September 1, 1963): 13.

121. J. T. Ngugi, "A Kenyan at the Conference," *Transition,* no. 5 (July 30, 1962): 7.

122. Ngugi wa Thiong'o, *Decolonizing the Mind: The Politics of Language in African Literature* (London; Nairobi: J. Currey; Heinemann Kenya [etc.], 1986), 22.

123. *Conference of African Writers of English Expression* (Kampala: Makerere University College, 1962), 5.

124. *Conference of African Writers of English Expression,* 94.

125. *Conference of African Writers of English Expression,* 103.

126. Gérard, *European-Language Writing in Sub-Saharan Africa,* 679.

127. Gérard, 683.

128. Kalliney, "Modernism," 340.

129. Kalliney, 341.

130. Cohn, *The Latin American Literary Boom and U.S. Nationalism during the Cold War,* 96.

131. Cohn, 93.

132. Wilford, *Mighty Wurlitzer,* 113.

133. Benson, *Black Orpheus,* 164.

134. Saunders, *Cultural Cold War,* 272.

135. Kalliney, "Modernism," 355.

136. Cohn, *Latin American Literary Boom,* 69.

137. *The American Negro Writer and His Roots: Selected Papers* (New York: American Society of African Culture, 1960).

138. Sarah Brouillette, "On the History of Global Cultural Policy," unpublished manuscript, 2017.

139. Sarah Brouillette, "UNESCO and the Book in the Developing World," *Representations* 127, no. 1 (2014): 37, doi:10.1525/rep.2014.127.1.33.

140. Andrew Rubin, *Archives of Authority: Empire, Culture, and the Cold War* (Princeton: Princeton University Press, 2012), 60.

141. Richardson and Fijałkowski, *Refusal of the Shadow*, 81.

142. Amílcar Cabral, *Return to the Source: Selected Speeches* (New York: Monthly Review Press, 1974), 43.

143. Fanon, *Wretched of the Earth*, 227.

144. "Cultural Diplomacy: The Linchpin of Public Diplomacy" (Washington, DC: Department of State Bureau of Public Affairs, September 27, 2011), 1, http://www.state.gov/pdcommission/reports/174096.htm.

145. "Cultural Diplomacy," 2.

146. As quoted in Benson, *Black Orpheus*, 36.

147. Benson, 36.

148. Edward W. Said, *Humanism and Democratic Criticism* (New York: Palgrave Macmillan, 2004), 38.

149. Phyllis Taoua, "The Effects of Censorship on the Emergence of Anti-Colonial Protest in France," *South Central Review* 32, no. 1 (2015): 50.

150. Taoua, 51.

151. Richardson and Fijałkowski, *Refusal of the Shadow*, 41.

152. Casanova, *The World Republic of Letters*, 12.

153. Casanova, 36.

3. Stubborn Nationalism: Example Two, Movement Literatures

1. Marjorie Perloff, "Whose New American Poetry? Anthologizing in the Nineties," *Diacritics* 26, no. 3 (1996): 104–23.

2. Jed Rasula, *The American Poetry Wax Museum: Reality Effects, 1940–1990* (Chicago: National Council of Teachers of English, 1996), 227.

3. Greg Barnhisel, "Perspectives USA and the Cultural Cold War: Modernism in Service of the State," *Modernism/Modernity* 14, no. 4 (2007): 729–30.

4. Loren Glass, *Counterculture Colophon: Grove Press, the Evergreen Review, and the Incorporation of the Avant-Garde* (Palo Alto, CA: Stanford University Press, 2013), 22.

5. Donald Allen, *The New American Poetry: 1945–1960* (Berkeley: University of California Press, 1960), xi.

6. William Carlos Williams and John C. Thirlwall, *The Selected Letters of William Carlos Williams* (New York: New Directions Publishing, 1957), 131.

7. James Smethurst, *The Black Arts Movement: Literary Nationalism in the 1960s and 1970s* (Chapel Hill: University of North Carolina Press, 2005), 55, 56.

8. Smethurst, 55.

9. Imamu Amiri Baraka, *The LeRoi Jones / Amiri Baraka Reader*, ed. William J. Harris (New York: Basic Books, 2000), 382.

10. Max Elbaum, *Revolution in the Air: Sixties Radicals Turn to Lenin, Mao and Che* (New York: Verso, 2002), 2.

11. M. McLaughlin, *The Long, Hot Summer of 1967: Urban Rebellion in America* (New York: Springer, 2014); Clay Risen, *A Nation on Fire: America in the Wake of the King Assassination* (Hoboken, NJ: Wiley, 2009).

12. Elbaum, *Revolution in the Air*, 4.

13. Glass, *Counterculture Colophon*, 31.

14. "Young Lords Party 13-Point Program and Platform," n.d., http://www2 .iath.virginia.edu/sixties/HTML_docs/Resources/Primary/Manifestos /Young_Lords_platform.html.

15. "Young Lords Party 13-Point Program and Platform."

16. Huey P. Newton, *War Against the Panthers: A Study of Repression in America* (Santa Cruz: University of California, Santa Cruz, 1980), 84.

17. Linda Harrison, "On Cultural Nationalism," *Black Panther* 2, no. 29 (1969): 6.

18. Amiri Baraka, "The Wailer," *Callaloo*, no. 23 (1985): 248.

19. Baraka, *The LeRoi Jones / Amiri Baraka Reader*, 369.

20. Baraka, 369.

21. Gloria Anzaldúa, *Borderlands / La Frontera: The New Mestiza* (San Francisco: Aunt Lute Books, 2007), 85.

22. Rodolfo Gonzales, *I Am Joaquin: An Epic Poem* (Denver: R. Gonzales, 1967), 3. "An gringo" is in original.

23. Gonzales, 11, 20.

24. Rodolfo Gonzales, *I Am Joaquín: Yo Soy Joaquín: An Epic Poem. With a Chronology of People and Events in Mexican and Mexican American History* (New York: Bantam Books, 1972), 3.

25. Rafael Pèrez-Torres, *Movements in Chicano Poetry: Against Myths, against Margins* (New York: Cambridge University Press, 1995), 47.

26. Walt Whitman, *Walt Whitman's Leaves of Grass* (New York: Oxford University Press, 2005), 27.

27. Langston Hughes, *The Collected Poems of Langston Hughes* (New York: Random House, 1995), 24, 190.

28. Joan Richardson, *Wallace Stevens: The Later Years, 1923–1955* (Garden City, NY: Beech Tree Books, 1988), 388.

29. John K. Young, *Black Writers, White Publishers: Marketplace Politics in Twentieth-Century African American Literature* (Jackson: University Press of Mississippi, 2010), 94.

30. Gwendolyn Brooks, *Report from Part One* (Detroit: Broadside Press, 1972), 86.

31. Brooks, 77.

32. James D. Sullivan, "Killing John Cabot and Publishing Black: Gwendolyn Brooks's 'Riot,'" *African American Review* 36, no. 4 (2002): 557–69.

33. Brooks, *Report from Part One,* 24.

34. Joyce Ann Joyce, *Conversations with Sonia Sanchez* (Jackson: University Press of Mississippi, 2007), 32–33.

35. Gwendolyn Brooks, *Riot* (Detroit: Broadside Press, 1969), 1.

36. "Africobra African Commune of Bad Relevant Artists," April 7, 2014, https://web.archive.org/web/20140407082018/http://africobra.com/Introduction.html.

37. Brooks, *Riot,* 9.

38. Brooks, 10.

39. Brooks, 11.

40. Brooks, 22.

41. Maya Angelou, *The Complete Collected Poems of Maya Angelou* (New York: Random House, 2009), 38.

42. Marilyn Chin, *The Phoenix Gone, the Terrace Empty: Poems* (Minneapolis: Milkweed Editions, 2009), 16.

43. Chin, 16.

44. Chin, 16.

45. Hugh Wilford, *The Mighty Wurlitzer: How the CIA Played America* (Cambridge: Harvard University Press, 2009), 200.

46. Mary Washington, *The Other Blacklist: The African American Literary and Cultural Left of the 1950s* (New York: Columbia University Press, 2014), 251.

47. Wilford, *Mighty Wurlitzer,* 213–14.

48. Carl Rown to John Davis, December 14, 1964, 8.31, AMSAC Papers, Moorland-Spingarn Center, quoted in Wilford, 216.

49. Washington, *Other Blacklist,* 256.

50. Roger Rapoport, "Meet America's Meanest Dirty Trickster," *Mother Jones,* April 1977.

51. James Brooks, Chris Carlsson, and Nancy J. Peters, eds., *Reclaiming San Francisco: History, Politics, Culture* (San Francisco: City Lights Books, 1998), 226.

52. William J. Maxwell, *F. B. Eyes: How J. Edgar Hoover's Ghostreaders Framed African American Literature* (Princeton: Princeton University Press, 2015), 26.

53. Joel Whitney, *Finks: How the CIA Tricked the World's Best Writers* (New York: OR Books, 2017), 123.

54. Frances Fox Piven and Richard Cloward, *Regulating the Poor: The Functions of Public Welfare* (New York: Knopf, 2012).

55. Joan Roelofs, *Foundations and Public Policy: The Mask of Pluralism* (Albany: State University of New York Press, 2012), 25.

56. Richard Gibson, "A No to Nothing," *Kenyon Review* 13, no. 2 (1951): 252.

57. Langston Hughes, *The Big Sea: An Autobiography* (New York: Macmillan, 1993), 228.

58. John Alfred Williams, *Beyond the Angry Black* (New York: Cooper Square Publishers, 1966), 53.

59. Charles Spurgeon Johnson and Elmer Anderson Carter, *Opportunity: Journal of Negro Life* (New York: National Urban League, 1933), 20.

60. Ann Douglas, *Terrible Honesty: Mongrel Manhattan in the 1920s* (New York: Farrar, Straus and Giroux, 1996), 330.

61. David Levering Lewis, ed., *The Portable Harlem Renaissance Reader* (Princeton: Penguin Classics, 1995), xxii.

62. Nathan Irvin Huggins, *Harlem Renaissance* (New York: Oxford University Press, 1971), 303.

63. Huggins, 303.

64. Barbara Foley, *Spectres of 1919: Class and Nation in the Making of the New Negro* (Champaign: University of Illinois Press, 2010), 76.

65. Foley, 77.

66. Karen Ferguson, *Top Down: The Ford Foundation, Black Power, and the Reinvention of Racial Liberalism* (Philadelphia: University of Pennsylvania Press, 2013), 1.

67. Ferguson, 173.

68. Roelofs, *Foundations and Public Policy*, 25.

69. Brad R. Tuttle, *How Newark Became Newark: The Rise, Fall, and Rebirth of an American City* (New Brunswick, NJ: Rutgers University Press, 2009), 179.

70. Imamu Amiri Baraka and Charlie Reilly, *Conversations with Amiri Baraka* (Jackson: University Press of Mississippi, 1994), 31.

71. Kirkpatrick Sale, *SDS* (New York: Vintage Books, 1974), 635.

72. Noliwe M. Rooks, *White Money / Black Power: The Surprising History of African American Studies and the Crisis of Race in Higher Education* (Boston: Beacon Press, 2006), 33.

73. Rooks, 55–56.

74. Roderick A. Ferguson, *The Reorder of Things: The University and Its Pedagogies of Minority Difference* (University of Minnesota Press, 2012), 6.

75. Ferguson, 40.

76. Jodi Melamed, *Represent and Destroy: Rationalizing Violence in the New Racial Capitalism* (Minneapolis: University of Minnesota Press, 2011), 34, 95.

77. Eric Bennett, "How Iowa Flattened Literature," *The Chronicle of Higher Education,* February 10, 2014, https://www.chronicle.com/article/How -Iowa-Flattened-Literature/144531.

78. Eric Bennett, *Workshops of Empire: Stegner, Engle, and American Creative Writing during the Cold War* (Iowa City: University of Iowa Press, 2015), 8.

4. Turn of the Twenty-First Century: The National Tradition

1. Arjun Appadurai, *Modernity at Large: Cultural Dimensions of Globalization* (Minneapolis: University of Minnesota Press, 1996), 19.

2. Fredric Jameson, *Postmodernism, or, The Cultural Logic of Late Capitalism* (Durham, NC: Duke University Press, 1991), 44.

3. Appadurai, *Modernity at Large,* 31.

4. Appadurai, 34.

5. Caren Irr, *Toward the Geopolitical Novel: U.S. Fiction in the Twenty-First Century* (New York: Columbia University Press, 2013), 10.

6. Irr, 8.

7. Irr, 8.

8. "IWP Fall Residency | The International Writing Program," accessed June 29, 2016, https://iwp.uiowa.edu/residency.

9. "EJournal USA: Multicultural Literature in the United States Today," Electronic Journal, February 4, 2009, https://photos.state.gov/libraries /korea/49271/dwoa_122709/Multicultural.pdf.

10. "EJournal USA," 36.

11. Pascale Casanova, *The World Republic of Letters* (Cambridge: Harvard University Press, 2004), 36.

12. George Clack, ed., *Writers on America* (Washington, DC: U.S. Department of State, Bureau of Information Programs, 2002), https://web-archive-2017.ait.org.tw/infousa/zhtw/DOCS/writers/homepage.htm.

13. George Clack, "Introduction: Writers on America," in Clack, *Writers on America.*

14. Naomi Shihab Nye, "This Crutch That I Love," in Clack, *Writers on America.*

15. See *National Endowment for the Arts Appropriations History,* accessed June 11, 2018, https://www.arts.gov/open-government/national-endowment-arts-appropriations-history.

16. Thane Peterson, "Beyond the 1990s' 'Culture Wars,'" Bloomberg.com, July 26, 2004, http://www.bloomberg.com/news/articles/2004-07-26/beyond-the-1990s-culture-wars.

17. Eleanor Wilner, "Poetry and the Pentagon: Unholy Alliance? By Eleanor Wilner," *Poetry* (October 2004), https://www.poetryfoundation.org/poetrymagazine/articles/detail/60444.

18. Andrew Carroll, *Operation Homecoming: Iraq, Afghanistan, and the Home Front, in the Words of U.S. Troops and Their Families, Updated Edition* (Chicago: University of Chicago Press, 2008), xi, xiv, xv.

19. Carroll, xiv.

20. Evans, "Free (Market) Verse," *The Baffler* 17 (2006): 25, http://www.thebaffler.com/salvos/free-market-verse.

21. Stephanie Strom, "Gaining a Starring Role in Utility Industry Deals," *New York Times,* September 26, 1995, sec. Business, http://www.nytimes.com/1995/09/26/business/gaining-a-starring-role-in-utility-industry-deals.html.

22. Kathryn Kranhold discusses this in "Big Electricity Trader Defaulted in June," *Wall Street Journal,* July 9, 1998, A2.

23. In "Bennington Means Business," a letter response in the *New York Times* (November 27, 1994), Barr takes responsibility for this decision.

24. Evans, "Free (Market) Verse," 27.

25. Evans, 28.

26. John Barr, "2006 Annual Letter: The Year in Review: The Poetry Foundation," Poetry Foundation, December 2006, http://www.poetryfoundation.org/foundation/annual-letter-2006.

27. Casanova, *World Republic of Letters,* 279.

28. Dana Gioia, *Can Poetry Matter? Essays on Poetry and Culture* (Minneapolis: Graywolf Press, 1992), 84.

29. "'American Life in Poetry' Reaches 1.5 Million Readers," Poetry Foundation, December 12, 2005, https://web.archive.org/web/20150906051156 /http://www.poetryfoundation.org/downloads/121205.pdf.

30. Ted Kooser and Steve Cox, *Writing Brave and Free: Encouraging Words for People Who Want to Start Writing* (Lincoln: University of Nebraska Press, 2006), 3.

31. Dana Gioia, "Title Tells All," *Poetry,* November 15, 2005, 45, 45, 47, 49.

32. Rita Dove, "Letter to the Editor," *Poetry* 184, no. 3 (2004): 248.

33. John Barr, "American Poetry in the New Century," *Poetry,* August 23, 2006, www.poetryfoundation.org/poetrymagazine/articles/detail/68634.

34. Barr.

35. Gioia, *Can Poetry Matter?* 10.

36. Joseph Epstein, "Who Killed Poetry?" *Commentary,* August 1988, 15.

37. John Barr, *Grace: An Epic Poem* (Pasadena, CA: Story Line Press, 1999), back cover.

38. Jill Singer, "So What Do You Do, John Barr?" mediabistro, March 23, 2004, http://www.mediabistro.com/So-What-Do-You-Do-John-Barr -a1356.html.

39. Barr, *Grace,* 11.

40. Barr, 11.

41. Barr, 11.

42. Barr, 15.

43. Barr, 41.

44. Barr, 75, 76.

45. Barr, 82.

46. John Barr and Michael Useem, "Poetry and Investment Banking: It's All about Risk," Knowledge@Wharton, January 26, 2005, http://knowledge .wharton.upenn.edu/article/poetry-and-investment-banking-its-all -about-risk/.

47. Barr and Useem.

48. Barr, *Grace,* 91.

49. Barr, back cover.

50. Kent Johnson, "Comment on 'Free (Market) Verse': Steve Evans on the Poetry Foundation and Conservative Politics / Aesthetics," *Montevidayo* (blog), November 17, 2011, http://montevidayo.com/2011/11/free-market-verse -steve-evans-on-the-poetry-foundation-and-conservative-politicsaesthetics/; Dana Goodyear, "The Moneyed Muse," *New Yorker,* February 19, 2007, http://www.newyorker.com/magazine/2007/02/19/the-moneyed-muse.

51. John Barr, *Opcit at Large* (Pasadena, CA: Red Hen Press, 2013).

52. Robert Frost, *The Poetry of Robert Frost: The Collected Poems, Complete and Unabridged* (New York: Macmillan, 2002), 348.

53. Robert Frost and Lawrance Roger Thompson, *Selected Letters* (New York: Holt, Rinehart and Winston, 1964), 228.

54. Jeff Westover, "National Forgetting and Remembering in the Poetry of Robert Frost," *Texas Studies in Literature and Language* 46, no. 2 (2004): 239.

55. Frost, *Poetry of Robert Frost,* 348.

56. Toni Morrison, "Comment," *New Yorker,* October 5, 1998, 32.

57. Miller Williams, *Some Jazz a While: Collected Poems* (Champaign: University of Illinois Press, 1999), 159.

58. Maya Angelou, *The Complete Collected Poems of Maya Angelou* (New York: Random House, 2009), 271.

59. Angelou, 271.

60. C. O. Grossman, "The 'Difficult Miracle' of State-funded Poetry," unpublished manuscript, 2016.

61. Angelou, *Complete Collected Poems,* 271.

62. Elizabeth Alexander, *Crave Radiance: New and Selected Poems 1990–2010* (Minneapolis: Graywolf Press, 2012), 249.

63. Richard Blanco, *One Today: A Poem for Barack Obama's Presidential Inauguration* (Pittsburgh, PA: University of Pittsburgh Press, 2013).

64. Richard Blanco, *For All of Us, One Today: An Inaugural Poet's Journey* (Boston: Beacon Press, 2013), 12.

65. Blanco, 91.

66. Harris Feinsod, "Glosses and Conjectures on the Inaugural Poem," ARCADE, January 28, 2013, http://arcade.stanford.edu/blogs/glosses-and -conjectures-inaugural-poem.

67. Blanco, *For All of Us,* 88.

68. Blanco, 88.

69. "American Corners Celebrate Black History Month," Wikileaks Public Library of US Diplomacy (Oman Muscat, April 6, 2005), https://search .wikileaks.org/plusd/cables/05MUSCAT561_a.html; "Cultural Envoy, Gina Loring, Inspires Social Activism Through Creative Writing," Wikileaks Public Library of US Diplomacy (Kuwait Kuwait City, February 24, 2008), https://search.wikileaks.org/plusd/cables /08KUWAIT216_a.html; "An Eventful Evening of African American Poetry in the Urals," Wikileaks Public Library of US Diplomacy (Russia

Yekaterinburg, March 2, 2009), https://search.wikileaks.org/plusd/cables
/09YEKATERINBURG13_a.html.

70. "Ms. Ilene Evans, African-American Storyteller, Performing Artist and
Singer Inspires Kuwaiti Audiences and Celebrates Black History Month
in Kuwait," Wikileaks Public Library of US Diplomacy (Kuwait Kuwait
City, March 19, 2009), https://wikileaks.org/plusd/cables/09KUWAIT259
_a.html.

71. "Program Evaluation: Hip Hop Trio Rocks Kuwait," Wikileaks Public
Library of US Diplomacy (Kuwait Kuwait City, April 18, 2007),
https://wikileaks.org/plusd/cables/07KUWAIT578_a.html.

72. "Ünlü Şarkıcıya Seyirci Şoku," Milliyet.com.tr, March 20, 2011,
http://www.milliyet.com.tr/unlu-sarkiciya-seyirci-soku/gundem
/gundemdetay/20.03.2011/1366722/default.htm.

73. "Reading Abroad: American Writers on Tour | International Writing
Program," accessed June 23, 2014, http://iwp.uiowa.edu/programs
/reading-abroad.

74. "IWP Advisory Committee | International Writing Program," accessed
August 12, 2014, http://iwp.uiowa.edu/about-iwp/advisory-committee.

75. Adrienne Rich, "Why I Refused the National Medal for the Arts," *Los
Angeles Times,* August 3, 1997, http://articles.latimes.com/1997/aug/03
/books/bk-18828.

76. Poets Against the War, April 8, 2011, https://poetsagainstthewar.org.

77. Vanessa Place, "The Death of the Text: Kenneth Goldsmith at the White
House," *Harriet: The Blog* (blog), accessed February 6, 2017, https://www
.poetryfoundation.org/harriet/2011/05/the-death-of-the-text-kenneth
-goldsmith-at-the-white-house/.

78. Place.

79. "Renga for Obama," *Harvard Review Online,* April 30, 2017, http://www
.harvardreview.org/?q=features/poetry/renga-obama.

80. Stefano Harney and Fred Moten, *The Undercommons: Fugitive Planning
and Black Study* (Brooklyn, NY: Minor Compositions, 2013), 32.

81. "National Universities Rankings," *US News and World Report,* n.d.,
http://colleges.usnews.rankingsandreviews.com/best-colleges/rankings
/national-universities?int=9ff208.

82. "IPEDS Data Center," accessed June 22, 2015, https://nces.ed.gov/ipeds
/datacenter/Default.aspx.

83. Susan Falcon, "The 2013–2014 Report on the Academic Job Market:
Adjunct Unions, Administrative Bloat, and Reform of Student Loans,"

Association of Writers and Writing Programs, November 2014, https://www.awpwriter.org/careers/career_advice_view/3604/the_2013-14 _report_on_the_academic_job_market_adjunct_unions_administrative _bloat_reform_of_student_loans.

84. Mark McGurl, *The Program Era: Postwar Fiction and the Rise of Creative Writing* (Cambridge: Harvard University Press, 2009), 410.

85. "The Equality of Opportunity Project," accessed December 14, 2017, http://www.equality-of-opportunity.org/college/.

86. "Equality of Opportunity Project."

87. Christopher Findeisen, "Injuries of Class: Mass Education and the American Campus Novel," *PMLA* 130, no. 2 (2015): 294, https://doi.org/10 .1632/pmla.2015.130.2.284.

88. "IPEDS Data Center."

89. William L Andrews, Frances Smith Foster, and Trudier Harris, *The Oxford Companion to African American Literature* (New York: Oxford University Press, 1997), 72.

90. "AWP Hallmarks of a Successful MFA Program in Creative Writing," accessed July 6, 2016, https://www.awpwriter.org/guide/directors_handbook _hallmarks_of_a_successful_mfa_program_in_creative_writing.

91. Eric Bulson, *Little Magazine, World Form* (New York: Columbia University Press, 2016), 14.

92. "Poetry for The People," accessed June 27, 2015, http://africam.berkeley .edu/content/poetry-for-the-people.

93. "Graywolf Press—GuideStar Profile," accessed December 20, 2017, https://www.guidestar.org/profile/91–1257237.

94. "About," Asian American Writers' Workshop, accessed February 6, 2017, http://aaww.org/about/.

95. "Cave Canem: Mission & History," accessed July 27, 2016, http:// cavecanempoets.org/mission-history/.

96. This is based on a random sample of around 600 books taken from the more than one million that *Books in Print* lists as published in the United States in English from 2000 to 2017.

97. Kathryn VanSpanckeren, *Outline of American Literature* (Washington, DC: U.S. Department of State, 1994), 136.

98. Roxane Gay, "Where Things Stand," Rumpus, June 6, 2012, http:// therumpus.net/2012/06/where-things-stand/.

99. Amiri (LeRoi Jones) Baraka, "The Revolutionary Theatre," *Liberator* 5 (1965): 4–6.

100. "Cave Canem: Mission and History."

101. Kenneth W. Warren, "You Tell Me It's the Institution: Creative Writing and Literary History," *Los Angeles Review of Books,* September 13, 2015, https://lareviewofbooks.org/article/you-tell-me-its-the-institution -creative-writing-and-literary-history/.

102. "Results from the Annual Arts Basic Survey (2013–2015) | NEA," accessed January 6, 2018, https://www.arts.gov/artistic-fields/research-analysis /arts-data-profiles/arts-data-profile-10.

103. "A Decade of Arts Engagement: Findings from the Survey of Public Participation in the Arts, 2002–2012" (Washington, DC: National Endowment for the Arts, January 2015), 69.

104. "How a Nation Engages with Art: Highlights from the 2012 Survey of Public Participation in the Arts" (Washington, DC: National Endowment for the Arts, September 2013), 24.

105. Thomas Franssen and Giselinde Kuipers, "Sociology of Literature and Publishing in the Early 21st Century: Away from the Centre," *Cultural Sociology* 9, no. 3 (2015): 291, https://doi.org/10.1177/1749975515594467.

106. "How a Nation Engages with Art," 24.

107. "Statement of Values," accessed January 17, 2017, http://dornsife.usc.edu /engl/statement-of-values/.

108. Scott Esposito, "The Art of a Nation Will Outlast Its Governments," *Literary Hub* (blog), December 19, 2016, http://lithub.com/the-art-of-a -nation-will-outlast-its-governments/.

109. Paula Moya, *The Social Imperative: Race, Close Reading, and Contemporary Literary Criticism* (Palo Alto, CA: Stanford University Press, 2015), 52.

110. Philip Metres and Mark Nowak, "Poetry as Social Practice in the First Person Plural: A Dialogue on Do," *Iowa Journal of Cultural Studies* 12 (2010): 14.

111. Metres and Nowak, 17.

112. Siddhartha Deb, "The Art of War," Baffler, April 6, 2017, https://thebaffler .com/contraband/the-art-of-war.

Conclusion

1. Élisée Reclus, "Art and the People," theyliewedie.org, accessed December 12, 2016, https://www.theyliewedie.org/ressources/biblio/en /Reclus,_Elisee_-_Art_and_the_people.html; "Situationist Manifesto," Situationist International Online, May 17, 1960, http://www.cddc.vt.edu /sionline/si/manifesto.html; George Murray, "For a Revolutionary Culture," *Black Panther Intercommunal News Service* 2, no. 5 (1968): 12.

2. Reclus, "Art and the People."

3. "Situationist Manifesto."

4. Murray, "For a Revolutionary Culture."

5. Kristin Ross, *Communal Luxury: The Political Imaginary of the Paris Commune* (New York: Verso Books, 2015), 14.

6. "Watts: Remember What They Built, Not What They Burned," *Los Angeles Times,* August 11, 2015, http://www.latimes.com/opinion/op-ed/la -oe-0811-kelley-watts-civil-society-20150811-story.html.

7. Ross, *Communal Luxury,* 54.

8. Harney and Moten, *Undercommons,* 30.

9. Harney and Moten, 42–43.

ACKNOWLEDGMENTS

I began this book because I received something called a "New Economy Grant." Thank you, New Economy donor; I cannot find your name anywhere anymore. The New Economy grant lasted about as long as the new economy, or not very long. I got the grant in 2000, to write a study of contemporary literature, the languages in which it is written, and globalization. So I began this book as a study of contemporary literature. I am ending it about fifteen years later as a historical study of, among other things, the particular literary formations that happened at the turn of the twenty-first century. Along the way I have accumulated a billion debts. I will attempt to list them, but I am sure to fail: Thank you, American Council of Learned Societies, for a fellowship that let me take a year's leave at Mills College. Thank you, University of Hawai'i at Manoa and Mills College and the Quigley Fund at Mills College, for various small grants along the way.

I started this book when I was still in Hawai'i. And it keeps some of the Hawai'i focus. I owe big debts to colleagues at University of Hawai'i at Manoa. Cynthia Franklin, Susan Schultz, and Rob Wilson all argued with early drafts of work that eventually became part of this book. But please do not hold them responsible for anything; the version here is a version of some work they read, but ten years later they are in no way responsible for its errors. I especially am grateful for a lasting friendship with Ida Yoshinaga, one full of provocation and recommended reading.

This project became historical when I moved to the Bay Area. And while there, I worked on this book while sitting next to Aaron Benanav, David Buuck, Joshua Clover, and Stephanie Young. So much gratitude for their quiet working in various coffee shops. Melissa Buzzeo read early drafts of this work and listened to me complain about it. Eirik Steinhoff read a version of a chapter and was amazingly helpful, so much so that his comments reshaped much of this project. Chris Chen gave me a list of around five books to read at just the right moment, and that list reframed the project. Buuck and Heriberto Yépez read late versions, argued with me, and caught some errors. Angelo Sphere, Lindsay Baille, and Camille Brown were great research assistants. Late in the process, twitter DM conversations with Sarah Brouillette and Greg Barnhisel were helpful, as were DMs with Julian Park.

Many of these ideas were argued out in emails with Jasper Bernes, Chris Chen, Joshua Clover, Tim Kreiner, and Wendy Trevino. Some of these ideas were developed out of pieces that appeared under the name Commune Editions (a name I share with Jasper and Joshua).

If the first part of this book is in debt to colleagues in Hawai'i, the second half is in debt to Stephanie Young and C. O. Grossman, the best and most tolerant co-conspirators ever.

Biggest debt of all, though, is to Ellen Feiss.

My work has also been widened by a rich constellation of writers who, because of the specificity of my concerns here (and my desire to write a fairly short book), do not show up in later chapters. Still, I should acknowledge that I am writing this with a big stack of influence beside my desk. Some of these writers came into my life by the lovely chances that friendships bring but beyond this are idiosyncratic. Two feel crucial in how much they shaped my thinking and yet do not get quoted in the book itself and so deserve special acknowledgment: Heriberto Yépez's *The Empire of Neomemory* and Joshua Clover's *1989: Bob Dylan Didn't Have This to Sing About*. I was typesetting Heriberto's book at a pivotal moment in the writing of this book. The three-part structure of his book and the way he embraces the potentially diversionary as not at all diversionary dramatically changed the structure of this book. I had dinner numerous times with Joshua while he was writing *1989*, and our conversations helped me turn to periodization more than I might have otherwise.

Also, thanks go to Bill Luoma and Charles Weigl and Sasha Spahr. They too should not be held responsible for any errors.

INDEX